D1171306

Emily Dickinson's Letters

TO DR. AND MRS. JOSIAH GILBERT HOLLAND

Emily Dickinson's Letters

TO DR. AND MRS. JOSIAH GILBERT HOLLAND

EDITED BY THEIR GRANDDAUGHTER
THEODORA VAN WAGENEN WARD

HARVARD UNIVERSITY PRESS
CAMBRIDGE, MASSACHUSETTS
1951

Second Printing

PRINTED AT THE HARVARD UNIVERSITY PRINTING OFFICE
CAMBRIDGE, MASSACHUSETTS, U.S.A.

PREFACE

Soon after the appearance of the first and second series of poems by Emily Dickinson in 1890 and 1891, the poet's sister, Lavinia, and her editor, Mabel Loomis Todd, began to collect as many of her letters as were available for publication. The collection was published in 1894 by Roberts Brothers of Boston in two small volumes under the title *Letters of Emily Dickinson.* Included in them were twenty-eight letters to my grandparents, Dr. and Mrs. Josiah Gilbert Holland. When an enlarged edition was published in 1931, Mrs. Todd added one more letter to the Hollands. These twenty-nine letters were only a small proportion of the number they had received, but at the time when my grandmother sent them to Mrs. Todd she believed that the larger group had not been preserved. She never had the pleasure of learning of her mistake, for it was not until thirty-three years after her death that her grandchildren found sixty of them which she had put away with other papers in a box in the attic. With the addition of four letters in the possession of other members of the family, they form a legacy which I have long desired to share with the public.

In order to make this record of Emily Dickinson's friendship with my grandparents as complete as possible, it has seemed desirable to reprint the already published letters, and I have also added two letters from Lavinia Dickinson.

Through this connected series of ninety-three letters from Emily Dickinson covering a period of more than thirty years, it is possible for the first time to observe her development during the whole of her adult life. Although the letters contain no startling revelations, they reflect the changes wrought in her by inner and outer experience, through which she grew from a gifted girl to a mature woman and a finished artist. Since none of them bears a date and no envelopes have been preserved, it has been difficult to arrange them in the exact order in which they were written. It is possible that a few errors have occurred in dating those that contain no reference to events, in spite of careful study of the handwriting and the papers on which they are written.

Owing to the unfortunate disappearance of the manuscripts of the published letters after they were returned to my grandmother, my study of them has been limited to the printed text. Even with this handicap I have ventured – in view of recorded dates in the Holland family and through internal evidence – to redate a number of the letters in this group. They are reprinted here exactly as they appear in the 1931 edition of *Letters of Emily Dickinson,* in which the punctuation and use of capitals conform to accepted usage. In presenting the hitherto unpublished letters, however, I have followed the punctuation of the manuscripts as closely as possible, sacrificing whatever advantage there may be in uniformity for the sake of preserving as much as possible of the peculiarly emphatic quality of the original script.

As a background for the letters I have written an introduction telling of the friendship that brought them into being. The outward events in the life of Emily Dickinson were few, and it has seemed best not to repeat here many aspects of it that have been extensively dealt with elsewhere. If undue emphasis seems to have been placed on the Hollands, it is because they are not well known today, and their intimate connection with the contents of the letters makes it desirable for the reader to become acquainted with their personal characteristics and some of the circumstances of their lives. In addition to the connecting links between the letters and the notes on historical and literary allusions and quotations, I have added for the benefit of those who are interested in the methods used in dating the letters a summary of my study of the handwriting as it changes from year to year and of the papers on which the letters are written.

A number of persons have contributed to the making of this book, and I offer my sincere thanks to friends and friendly strangers who have helped to accumulate information for it. To George F. Whicher, Professor of English at Amherst College, who gave me access to his notes for *This Was a Poet,* and assisted me greatly in the initial stages of dating the letters, I am very grateful. As a novice in the field of scholarship I have benefited from the advice and guidance of William H. McCarthy, Jr., formerly of Houghton Library at Harvard University, whose vision of what the book should be enlarged my own conception of it, and whose unflagging interest and stimulating criticism have contributed largely to its realization.

Contents

Illustrations

THE BACKGROUND

They shut me up in prose —
As when, a little girl,
They put me in the closet
Because they liked me "still."

"Still!" Could themselves have peeped
And seen my brain go round,
They might as wise have lodged a bird
For treason in the pound!

Himself has but to will,
And, easy as a star,
Look down upon captivity
And laugh. Nor more have I!

Attempting to confine Emily Dickinson within the limits of the time and place in which she lived is like trying to catch the wind in a net. But winds have special characteristics, varying according to the direction from which they blow, and come laden with odors from the ground they have passed over. An east wind blowing across salt marshes differs markedly from a westerly breeze that has ruffled a field of clover as it passed.

Emily Dickinson's imagination reached out to wide horizons and her intuition plumbed the depths far below the personal, bringing to her poetry a universal quality that induces readers of the most divergent views to claim her as their own, yet nineteenth century New England flavored all she wrote. The conciseness of her expression, her choice of words, the hymnbook meters she used, were all characteristic of the particular culture into which she was born. Spontaneous and original in its deviation from the standards of the day, her writing was like a fresh shoot springing from the base of an old tree. Her unique mind followed its own course, but the direction of that course was set at a time when the village academies were adding science to the classics, and Puritanism was being infused with the doctrines of Emerson.

Regard for time and place is essential to an understanding of Emily Dickinson's life. Readers of a later generation, seeking an explanation for her withdrawal from society, may have failed to notice how little her seclusion mattered to those who knew her. It was, for her, a way of living, not a renunciation of life. She was not the only New England woman who gradually retired from community life and remained within her home. Local gossip was hardly more concerned with the secluded one than with those who remained in public view, for freedom to be singular was one of the privileges granted to New Englanders.

Emily Dickinson was never wholly a recluse. For twenty years she traveled no farther than her garden, but she continued to participate – on her own terms – in the life around her. In her girlhood she had taken part in all the activities of a happy group of young people. In spite of her special quality of timelessness, she maintained throughout her life warm friendships with men and women who represented their own time and fulfilled the conditions demanded of them by the society in which their roots were planted. That she did not feel alien to them is evident in the very profusion of the letters she wrote to those who drew her interest or affection. Among the chosen few to whom she wrote with special freedom and intimacy were Josiah and Elizabeth Holland.

When Thomas Wentworth Higginson first saw the *Letters of Emily Dickinson* in print in November 1894, he wrote to the editor, Mabel Loomis Todd, with whom he had collaborated in editing the poems, "Emilie has arrived. . . The editing so far seems admirable; I only doubted whether there were not too much of the earlier letters – not those to Austin which are infinitely valuable with their wealth of heart – still more shown in the letters to the Hollands." The special quality which Colonel Higginson found in those letters to my grandparents may be felt even more strongly in the larger group printed for the first time in this volume. The letters themselves make it clear that these two were important to Emily Dickinson, but one must look elsewhere to discover why she was drawn to them and what qualities in them held so much value for her.

I am handicapped in trying to build up a picture of my grandparents by the fact that I never knew my grandfather, who died long before I was born, and that my memories of my grandmother are those of a very small child, for I was only five at the time of her death. Aside from the impressions I received from family memories that I have heard recounted, my only first-hand material consists of some of my grandfather's letters to his wife and children, a few from my grandmother to her daughter Kate – my mother – and an early one from each of them to my grandfather's parents. For further information I have had to depend on Dr. Holland's published works, and the books and articles that have been written about him. These last tell the story of his life, but the portrait of the man in them is obscured by the portrayal of a public figure.

Dr. Holland's position is the strange one of a man who achieved wide popularity and exerted a strong influence during his life, but was completely forgotten within a few years after his death, except by those who knew him or who had been directly influenced by his writing. The taste of today finds little of interest in the poems, novels, and editorials which comprise his published work, and one wonders, after reading his lectures, what it was that drew out large and enthusiastic audiences to hear them on cold winter nights.

The first of the two books about him, published thirteen years after his death, was written by an old friend of the family, Mrs. H. M. Plunkett of Pittsfield, who stated in the preface that the writing of it was undertaken "to perpetuate the memory of a man whose name was for many years a household word." The book is a tribute to a personal friend by a contemporary who admired his character and achievement and to a large extent shared his views. Thus the reader sees him closely through the eyes of his own generation, but is confined to a limited perspective.

The second book, published in 1940 by Harry Houston Peckham, attempts to evaluate the man and his work by considering him "both as a phenomenon and as an influence in relation to his times and his social and intellectual background." Mr. Peckham's special interest is to give Dr. Holland a place of importance in the history of American culture because of his influence on the popular thought of his time. In spite of this estimate of his value, however, the author seems unable to rid himself of the impression that as an individual the good doctor was a Calvinistic prig. In neither of these books is anything said about Mrs. Holland beyond the fact that she was a charming young woman when Dr. Holland married her, and that she became a devoted wife with a practical turn of mind which greatly assisted her husband in his career. All this has little bearing on why Emily Dickinson chose these two as her friends.

Before they can become alive for us as individuals, they must first be seen as members of the closely woven society of the region in which they lived. During the nineteenth century, the Connecticut Valley towns in western Massachusetts had an integrated life of their own. Springfield, Northampton, Amherst, and a dozen small towns that lay around them were inhabited largely by the descendants of the early settlers, and their families were linked together by intermarriage and common customs. In pioneer days a hundred miles of uninhabited forest had lain between the valley and its parent colony on Massachusetts Bay. Even in my grandparents' time something of this separateness lingered, but the people of the region were in easy contact with the outside world, turning quite as readily toward New York as toward Boston for their cultural associations. Their way of living still had a rural quality, but on the solid foundation that had been laid by the earlier generations, a satisfying social life had grown up. Solomon Bulkley Griffin, writing of Springfield in the first half of the nineteenth century, said, "Larger recognition was given to the cultivated side of life, and those who paid heed to the amenities were highly regarded. So came a recognized aristocracy of education, brains and social accomplishment."

My grandmother's family, the Chapins, had taken part in the development of the Connecticut Valley from the earliest days of the settlement. In 1635 permission was given simultaneously to the inhabitants of several towns in the Massachusetts Bay Colony to emigrate to sites along the Connecticut River. Settlers from Roxbury chose for the site of their new home a spot which the Indians called Agawam, but they soon renamed it Springfield. A year after it was founded, Samuel Chapin joined the settlement. He was a man of strong character and soon became a leader in the community, exercising authority as a magistrate, and influence as deacon of the church to the end of his long life. A monument in his honor, designed by Augustus Saint-Gaudens and erected in 1887 as part of a project in memory of the founders of Springfield, shows the typical figure of the Puritan in flowing cloak and high-crowned hat, carrying a Bible.

Among the early generations of Chapins, boys were so abundant that the countryside became peopled with families of that name. Elizabeth Chapin's father, Whitfield Chapin, had grown up in one of the numerous Chapin homesteads that lined both sides of the road from Springfield to Chicopee, four miles to the north, but as a young man he moved into Springfield and became a partner in a lumber business. When he died in 1833, leaving a large family, his widow found it hard to meet the needs of her growing children. Elizabeth, who was ten at the time of her father's death, was taken into the home of an uncle in Albany where she was given a good education at the Albany Female Academy, a school of high standing at that time.

In Albany Elizabeth found a different social environment from the one in which she had spent her childhood. The aristocratic system of the early Dutch settlers formed the background of society in the New York state capital, and the descendants of the Patroons still owned vast estates in the surrounding country. Social classes remained distinct, and the family with whom Elizabeth lived joined in the gaieties of the holidays which were celebrated according to Dutch custom, and dispensed charity to the poor as members of the upper class. Elizabeth formed close ties with this happy household, but she remained with them only through her school years. As the eldest daughter, she was needed at home as soon as her education was completed, and so, while still under twenty, she returned to the less sophisticated life of Springfield.

In spite of the difficulties involved in travel in those days, the people of the Connecticut Valley towns visited one another frequently. It is not surprising, therefore, that Josiah Holland first saw Elizabeth Chapin at a party in Northampton in the winter of 1843–1844. He admired her from a distance all the evening, but was not introduced to her, and it was not until several months later that he met her in Springfield, where he had just settled to start the practice of medicine. They were both active in the affairs of the South Church (Congregational), where they had frequent opportunities to be together. The courtship followed the regular pattern of the day, and they were married on the seventh of October 1845, at the home of Elizabeth's uncle in Albany.

According to the popular view, Josiah and Elizabeth Holland formed an ideal couple because of their opposite temperaments and contrasting physical characteristics. Like many of the Chapin women, my grandmother was small in body but forceful in spirit. She was vivacious and brisk, though always gracious in manner. Part of her charm lay in her directness and candor, and she was endowed with the strong feeling for reality often known as common sense. In contrast to her short stature and fair coloring, her husband's tall, erect figure, black eyes, and straight black hair gave him what one of his friends described as the appearance of an Indian chief. Together with his natural dignity, he had a simple and warmly responsive manner, the expression of a genuine interest in people.

Josiah Holland had reached this point in his life by a very different road from the one his wife had traveled. Though he also was descended from early settlers in the Massachusetts Bay Colony, his family had never established itself long enough in one place to become identified with it and did not settle in the Connecticut Valley until late in the eighteenth century. This tendency to move on had reached its climax in Harrison Holland, the father of Josiah, who wandered from one small town to another, taking with him little but a Puritanical piety, an inventive mind, and a childlike faith in the future. Josiah happened to be born in Belchertown, a few miles from Amherst, but he and his brothers and sisters while still children experienced all the jolts and jars that are involved in constantly making a new start, as the family moved from place to place seeking a better living. For a time their father carried on a fairly successful business in making parts for wheels to be sold to carriage makers. Sometimes the family lived on faith alone while their father perfected one of his inventions in a corner of the kitchen; sometimes he earned a bare living from the production of such homemade wares as pill boxes and buttons for cows' horns. The girls added to the family income by plaiting straw for hats, and for a time Josiah was obliged to leave school and work in a woolen mill. The public benefited from Harrison Holland's inventions far more than he did, for he never obtained a patent, and his ideas were taken up by others who were able to use them to better advantage. Mrs. Plunkett tells us that as late as 1894, when her book was written, raw silk from China still came wound on reels made from his design.

When the family reached Northampton, Josiah took matters into his own hands, found a job as chore boy in the house of a prominent citizen, went to high school, and began to prepare himself to fulfill the destiny which Mrs. Plunkett tells us he had always known was his — to be "an educated gentleman." That this boyish ambition was by no means a matter of externals is shown in the reminiscences of a friend of his early years which appeared in the *Springfield Republican* at the time of his death. The two boys had often spent nights together at each other's house, and his friend recalled one cold winter morning when Josiah stood half-dressed in the unheated bedroom, his face radiant with enthusiasm, a shoe in one hand and a copy of Thomson's *Seasons* in the other, reading aloud passages from the poem with a running commentary of appreciative analysis.

Josiah wanted to be a professional man. His upbringing would have inclined him toward the church, but he could not afford the years of study that were needed to prepare him for the ministry. He was not attracted to the law, but the medical profession appealed to him because of its direct relation to people's needs. Since only two years' training was required at that time, he decided to become a physician. Following customary procedure, he studied in the office of two prominent doctors in Northampton; and to qualify for the medical degree, he completed his course with two short terms of lectures at the Berkshire Medical College at Pittsfield.

The title "Doctor" clung to Josiah Holland all his life, though he soon dropped the practice of medicine. The most noteworthy fact that is remembered about him as a physician is his strong belief in fresh air at a time when the sick were closeted with their diseases and protected from the light of day. He had lost three sisters, two by tuberculosis, and he was so thoroughly convinced that a life in the open air would have saved them that when he married he took his young wife with him in his buggy wherever he went, to build up her health. But as a doctor he was a failure, chiefly because he was more interested in writing verses than in dosing his patients. Struggling against the cramping effects of poverty, he had early sought enlightenment and satisfaction for his aesthetic longings in the few books that were available to him, and his desire to expand his spirit through things of beauty became a part of the pattern of his life. In his efforts to educate himself he had learned to think independently, and his active mind not only craved an outlet but required a moral purpose for its expression.

As a minister he would have given his message ably to a limited group. As it was, each experimental step he took pushed him a little farther toward the position he was to achieve as lay preacher to a nationwide audience. He started a weekly paper which failed after a few months; then, feeling that a married man should earn an assured income, he turned to teaching. In 1847 he took a position in a business college at Richmond, Virginia, and the following year went to Vicksburg, Mississippi, as superintendent of schools. From Vicksburg in January 1848 he wrote a lively account of the seventeen-day journey from Springfield and addressed it to Samuel Bowles, the young editor of the *Springfield Daily Republican,* who printed it in three installments in an important column of the paper.

Vicksburg at that time was a raw, straggling town with a fluctuating population, and according to a letter which Dr. Holland wrote to his father, it was known in the north chiefly as "the place where they hung the gamblers." For the Hollands, life in Vicksburg was as strange as they would have found it in a foreign land, and their work there took on the guise of a missionary enterprise. Since the public school system of Mississippi had been established only two years, Dr. Holland undertook to organize and grade the schools on the plan Horace Mann had just put into effect in Massachusetts. He acted also as principal of the largest school, in which he found ninety undisciplined boys of all ages and conditions, while his wife taught a primary school to add a little to the modest salary he received. Mrs. Holland wrote home to her mother-in-law that even though she was enjoying the February flowers, she would not care permanently to exchange the southern winter with her native climate with its long freezing months. She criticized the economy of the southern agricultural system with the practical comment, "When corn and grain grow with such luxuriance here, it seems strange and foolish that they should all run mad about cotton, and not raise vegetables and stock enough to supply the market decently."

A vacation spent on a large plantation in Louisiana gave them an opportunity to observe another phase of southern life, and every new experience added to the fund of ideas which Dr. Holland felt impelled to put on paper. In spite of the demanding nature of his work, he found time for his writing, and sent some of his poems to magazines. Two poems of twelve stanzas each, with editorial comments praising them, were published in 1849 in the *Home Journal,* a New York periodical edited by N. P. Willis.

When the fatal illness of Mrs. Holland's mother brought them back to Springfield in the spring of 1849, Dr. Holland found an opening in the field of work most congenial to him. Mrs. Plunkett tells that while still at Vicksburg he had sent to the *Springfield Republican* a series of articles entitled "Sketches of Plantation Life," and that these probably led to his being asked to fill the post made vacant by the death of the associate editor shortly before his return. The articles were not published under that title, however, but appeared anonymously as "Three Weeks on a Cotton Plantation" some months after Dr. Holland had become a member of the staff. His connection with the paper came as suddenly as young love in a fairy tale. Many years later he told the story of his arrival in Springfield – how, on driving down the street from the station, he saw Samuel Bowles standing at the entrance to the *Republican* office, and how the same thought flashed through the minds of both. Action followed at once, and when Mr. Bowles asked him to fill the vacant position, the young man who had tried to be a doctor and a school teacher, but who never could keep from writing, accepted the offer instantly.

The daily *Republican* was then five years old. In 1844, when Samuel Bowles, Jr., persuaded his father to turn his weekly paper into a daily, he made some innovations which developed this small town sheet into a paper of national repute. Political news and comment and a pronounced stand on matters of national importance superseded the items of local interest, bits of general information, timetables, and advertisements of patent medicines that had formed the principal part of the earlier paper. Now, by asking Dr. Holland to join him, Mr. Bowles brought in an element that broadened the scope of the paper still more and added to its popularity not only in western Massachusetts, but in other parts of the country as well. As associate editor, Dr. Holland entered at once into the task of opening up for the common man opportunities to broaden his mind and enrich his soul. He added more extensive book reviews and other cultural articles to the paper, together with editorial essays on manners and morals in public and personal life.

The conduct of life was always supremely important to New Englanders, who had looked chiefly to the ministers for leadership in moral and social questions. But the beginnings of modern scientific thought were bringing changes into their lives which made the guidance of the local pulpits seem inadequate. The little sermons that came to them now as editorials in this daily paper were written from a fresh point of view by a young man who drew his ideas directly from his own observations and experience of life. There was a robust quality in his writing which was free from the sanctimonious platitudes of the pulpit. Under the humorous comment that often gave a trivial surface to the matter, one felt the convictions of this man who loved God with the same fervor with which his ancestors had feared Him. He loved life also, because life was good if one obeyed the laws of a generous Creator who wanted His children to be happy.

Josiah Holland himself was a happy man. His family life was one of rare harmony both within itself and in relation to its environment. There was a warmth and a sense of freedom in it that was lacking in many a New England home. Something of the Puritan still lived in the habits of thought of this couple, to be modified only as their field of experience broadened, but as I try to recapture their life I find in it also a quality of naturalness and spontaneity which kept it always fresh and vivid. It was undoubtedly this side of my grandfather's nature that brought him close to his readers and gave his words so much significance for them. His moral principles were as unyielding as an outcrop of rock in a New England pasture; but within the bounds which they imposed, his spirit flowered freely and innocently.

Through his articles in the *Republican* Dr. Holland began to receive invitations to speak in churches, in schools, and at civic functions. His popularity seems to have grown rapidly, for as early as 1854 the *Boston Advertiser* mentioned him as one of the special attractions of the coming lecture season in a list which included the names of Oliver Wendell Holmes, Bayard Taylor, and George William Curtis.

His first public honor came at Amherst, where, on the fifteenth of August 1851, he received the honorary degree of A.M. from Amherst College. On this occasion he was almost certainly invited to the house of Edward Dickinson, Emily's father, who, as treasurer of the college and a leading citizen, took an active personal interest in such events. He was already known to the Dickinson family through his writing in the *Springfield Republican* of which they were constant readers. What Emily at twenty thought of his writing we do not know, but it is certain that as a person he won a warm response from her. If their first meeting was at the Amherst commencement of 1851, Elizabeth Holland would not have been with them, for her eldest daughter was born shortly after that date. Following that occasion, Dr. Holland visited Amherst a number of times in connection with his work on the paper, and seems to have become acquainted with the whole Dickinson family before his wife had an opportunity to meet them. When she did, two years later, it was as Emily said "to love for aye."

It is possible that the families had been acquainted in earlier generations, for Emily Dickinson's forebears had also lived in the Connecticut Valley from the earliest years of its settlement. Nathaniel Dickinson, who came from England at about the same time as Samuel Chapin, migrated from the Massachusetts Bay Colony with the folk from Watertown who established themselves in the vicinity of Hartford and later moved up the river to settle Hadley. When East Hadley became a town in its own right and was given the name Amherst, the Dickinsons took part in building it up and always remained among its active citizens. Emily's grandfather, Samuel Fowler Dickinson, the first Dickinson lawyer, devoted himself to public welfare and was the leading spirit in the founding of Amherst College. He received the courtesy title "Squire," which his son Edward held after him, assuming also responsibility for the development of the college his father had started. Edward Dickinson's interest in public affairs took him into both the legislature and the senate of the Commonwealth of Massachusetts and for one term into the House of Representatives of the United States.

Emily Dickinson's father was the central figure in her home. He was a man to whose memory the words "dignity" and "integrity" naturally cling. Straight-backed, unyielding, and handsome, after the ascetic New England pattern, he was so reserved that a word of affection from him caused his children embarrassment. His individual soul was his own responsibility, and he was too proud — or too honest — to join the church until some inner call demanded it when he was a man in middle years. His life was so well-ordered and disciplined that he concealed from all but those who knew him most intimately the sensitive and fiery nature that lay within. In his own house he was like a central pillar of stone supporting the structure. His wife, small and gentle, lived but to carry out his wishes and to make the machinery of his home run smoothly. There were three children, William Austin, who became the third in line of the Dickinson lawyers, Emily, and Lavinia. While the family were deeply devoted to one another, and the young people lived a normal social life in the community, their way of living was tempered by the austerity of the father whose character formed its background.

In 1853, when Emily and her sister Lavinia first visited the Hollands in their home in Springfield, Dr. Holland had passed his thirty-fourth birthday, and his wife was thirty. Emily, who was approaching twenty-three, was enough younger to find exhilaration in the society of this couple whose experience of life exceeded hers and whose relation to each other must have looked like the ideal one for which every girl hopes. In their close mutual dependence, throughout the years that followed, the Hollands kept the brightness of their admiration for each other undimmed, and Dr. Holland's letters to his wife contain such passages as the following, which concludes a letter written in Utica, New York, the twenty-seventh of January 1867:

> They think a good deal of you at the Warrens', which of course is all very marvellous to me. It is not strange that I love you, but it is strange that when I love you so entirely there should be enough left for anybody else to hang an affection upon.

Although Mrs. Holland's personality was distinct, her interests were close to those of her husband, and her life was completely fulfilled in the activities that centered in her home. She was a good and thrifty housekeeper, and during the earlier years of her marriage she not only patched and darned, but made her own clothes and some of her husband's. She shared her home with Dr. Holland's widowed mother and her own younger sister, took care of her babies, and was her husband's best adviser on important decisions.

In all this she shared the ideals and performed the functions of the typical good housewife of her day, but everything she did was marked by an individual quality which Emily Dickinson thought of as birdlike. This came as much from the quickness of her mind as from the nimbleness of her small body. A characteristic that must have endeared her especially to Emily was her ability to lift the drab or the ponderous into a lighter atmosphere. The few persons still living who remember her speak of the wit of her conversation and the independence of her judgments. She had a strong sense of justice and of the rights of others, and could dart into the heart of a human problem as a hummingbird darts into the heart of a flower. She had the gift of meeting people on their own ground, yet retaining her own individuality in complete naturalness. She could be crisply outspoken, but never bitter, and her quick humor saved many an awkward situation.

In spite of the fullness of Mrs. Holland's days, she always had time for her friends, and the Hollands' parlor was a center where new books were shared and discussed and music was a part of the daily life. Everyone agreed that "Doctor" had an exceptionally fine tenor voice, and while he used it only to the glory of God on Sunday, on weekdays he sang the old ballads with equal enthusiasm. His wife may have accompanied him on the square piano, for she knew all the songs he sang; and one of my own few recollections of her is of perching on her little lap while she sang to me in a thin old voice the ballad about Lord Lovell, with all the verses accurately remembered down to the last sad twining of the rose-vines above the graves of the lovers.

The Hollands' three children, Annie, Kate, and Theodore, found companionship with their parents as natural as their unrestricted play. Perhaps Katie was punished for burning holes in her pinafore while smoking sweet-fern cigarettes, but she was not restrained from sliding down the banisters to attend family prayers. The behavior of the children was not always exemplary, but their mother knew how to handle them. Seeing trouble brewing between her two little girls, with a laugh and a quick word of rebuke she would curb the

flashing temper of the tormented one and at the same time disarm the tormentor.

Their father craved the affection of his children, and found his greatest pleasure in the companionship of his family. "When Father was sick," my mother told me, "he wanted the whole family around him." He was apt to dramatize his illnesses because they provided occasions when he could thoroughly enjoy his family's devotion, although he was able to laugh about it afterwards. His wife, however, who endured much pain from a disease of the eyes, so minimized her suffering and adjusted her life to impaired vision that it was simply accepted and seldom commented upon in the family. Her fortitude is more clearly seen by reflection in the letters that Emily wrote to her than through the memories that have been passed on to me. She was too busy with the concerns and the happiness of her little circle to make much of her disability.

At the Hollands' no one was afraid to laugh, and if the theater was still without the pale along with prize-fights and horse-racing, it did not matter much, because the theater hardly presented a problem to the inhabitants of western Massachusetts, and there were plenty of things at home to laugh about. A visit to the Hollands brought to Emily Dickinson in her early twenties a special release of spirit that infused her days with a glow for a long time afterward.

The Hollands afforded the stimulus, but the glow was Emily's own, for the excitement she felt in the companionship of her new friends was tinged with the luster of a lover's delight. Endowed with an extraordinary capacity for feeling, Emily loved intensely all her life, from dreaming adolescence to rich maturity. The great stream of her emotional force was fed by the earth itself, with its manifold forms of life, and by the spiritual realities she found behind the physical forms. Loving life in all its manifestations, her love for individual men and women was highly selective and confined to those few whom she found able to share or to enhance her own vital experience of sense and thought. To these — especially in the intensely personal years of youth — she poured out her affection with such abundance that they sometimes found the weight too heavy to carry. That the friendship with Mrs. Holland was sustained through more than thirty years was probably due in good part to the older woman's balanced nature, which enabled her to guide the flood of Emily's affection into the channels of loyalty and understanding.

While the friendship grew through the years, many changes came into the life of the Holland family. The *Springfield Republican* did not long absorb Dr. Holland's full energies, for his interest in writing demanded wider scope than journalism could offer. His first novel, *The Bay-Path,* a story of the early settlers in Springfield, was published in 1857, and was followed the next year by *Bitter-Sweet,* a narrative poem of New England life which gained such popularity that it is said to have sold in larger numbers than any other American poem except *Hiawatha.* In his review of it in the *Atlantic Monthly,* Lowell said:

> It is not free from faults of taste nor a certain commonplaceness of metre, but Mr. Holland always saves himself in some expression so simply poetical, some image so fresh and natural, the harvest of his own heart and eye, that we are ready to forgive him all his faults in our thankfulness at finding the soul of Theocritus transmigrated into the body of a Yankee. . . We mean it as very high praise when we say that *Bitter-Sweet* is one of the few

books that have found the secret of drawing up and assimilating the juices of this New World of ours.

The poems and novels that followed were widely read and as enthusiastically received by the general public as they were neglected or pulled apart by the critics. Realistic rather than romantic in conception, his stories, both in prose and verse, formed for many of his readers a link between literature and life, and introduced to them views that were just enough broader than theirs to lead them on to better reading. A special correspondent, writing to the *Chicago Tribune,* the twentieth of October 1881, shortly after his death, said:

> Less than half a century ago there was not considered sufficient material for a tolerable work of fiction in this country, and J. G. Holland was prominent in producing an interest in themes and subjects drawn entirely from American scenes and events.

By 1865 Dr. Holland had become a highly successful author and popular lecturer, receiving not only applause but abundant material rewards as well. His was the kind of success story that Americans have always loved, and the fact that the subject of it was a moralist made it especially attractive to many of his own generation. In part, it is the story of a man who happened to be on hand to meet a need which he was peculiarly fitted to fill, but it is also a story of an inner drive, frugal habits, and hard work, in all of which his wife's share was equal to his own.

Because of the poverty from which he suffered as a boy, the benefits of material wealth held great value for Dr. Holland, and his pleasure in obtaining them went hand in hand with his desire to be a force for good in the world. He enjoyed the results of his labor, not because of the power or social position wealth could give him, but because the advantages it brought seemed to him a part of the good life to which he believed every man was entitled. He was sustained through the hardships of his long lecture tours not only by the thought that he had a message for his hearers, but by the fact that he was making a hundred dollars a day to provide his family with all that he had missed as a child. When he could afford to be lavish, he delighted in spending money to improve his home, buying furniture, books and pictures, fast-trotting horses and smart carriages. But it was not only for his home that he spent freely. He was quite as free, and far more unwise, in his philanthropies. A friend said of him, "More frauds got money out of Dr. Holland than any man I ever knew. He could not believe that anyone was base enough to deceive him, so his hand was constantly dealing out money to the deserving and the undeserving alike."

It must be acknowledged, too, that he took great satisfaction in the acclaim of the public, but always with a kind of humble wonderment that he, Josiah Holland, had been given grace to stir the souls of the people and excite their admiration. He wrote to his wife, at the height of his popularity as a lecturer:

> Scranton, Pa. Nov. 22, 1871
>
> I am grateful that I had the grace to write this lecture, and that I have had the choice privilege of reading it to so many people. I am full of the sweet satisfaction of being an influence, gratefully and sometimes tearfully recognized, for good in the world. . . They thronged around me after lecture, and called this morning, and loitered on the corners of the streets to talk. They evidently felt that they had got hold of something worth talking about. There is only one drawback on my exquisite enjoyment of all this, and that is my absence from you and home.

The last decade of Dr. Holland's life was spent in New York, where he and his family went to live when he became founder and editor of the magazine, *Scribner's Monthly*. His flair for knowing what the public wanted, added to his experience both as editor and writer, made the magazine his most important and lasting achievement. The warmth of his relations with his business associates created a family atmosphere in the offices of *Scribner's Monthly* which even the contributors shared. Rebecca Harding Davis wrote to him that the tact and cordiality with which he rejected a manuscript left the author quite as satisfied as if he had accepted it. His sympathy for struggling young writers sometimes forced members of his staff to check his generous impulses in order to maintain the standards he had set for the magazine. Robert Underwood Johnson remembered hearing him say to the assistant editor, Richard Watson Gilder, "I do believe, Gilder, that you have an antipathy to anyone who wants to write for this magazine."

Dr. Holland's humanity always remained broader than his intellectual outlook. He might disagree with the views of his friends, but he had a firm belief in the right of every man to think for himself. At the time of his death, in 1881, his friend Edward Eggleston said:

> He was orthodox in his belief, and never crossed the line between orthodoxy and heterodoxy; occasionally he looked over the fence longingly; sometimes he had his feet on the lower rails; and once in a while he almost got one foot over, but he never really crossed the fence; but he would have died rather than that any man who as a matter of conviction wanted to go over should be deterred from doing so.

During all these years the contact between Emily Dickinson and Elizabeth Holland was never broken. Although Emily's visits to Springfield ceased after the early years, my grandmother often went to Amherst, and from 1853 until shortly before Emily's death in 1886 they continued to write to each other. The arrival of each letter from Emily was an occasion of excitement for the whole family. Because of their mother's impaired sight, one of the girls usually read the letters aloud, and my mother became expert in deciphering the strongly individual handwriting, even though some of Emily's expressions were beyond her understanding. Frequently there were poems enclosed. One would like to feel that the Hollands recognized Emily's genius, but their taste was too limited by the conventional forms of their time to enable them to see the full worth of her poetry. Dr. Holland is quoted as having said that Emily's verse was too ethereal for publication, and the personal nature of Mrs. Holland's feeling may have obscured her appreciation of the artist in her friend. Her poetry was set apart, as something special, not to be judged according to recognized standards, but warmly cherished as the individual expression of her stimulating, elusive, affectionate self.

After she passed thirty-five, Emily never left home, but the quality of her living lost none of its vividness, becoming more concentrated as she drew the boundaries closer. Her chosen friends found that the wall she gradually built to shield her from the outside world offered them no obstruction. She welcomed every contact with Mrs. Holland and eagerly anticipated her visits. In addition to the visits they made at the Dickinsons', the Hollands were often in Amherst during the decade beginning in 1865 to visit Mrs. Holland's cousins the Seelyes. Henrietta Chapin of Albany had married Laurenus Clark Seelye when he was pastor of the North Church in Springfield; shortly after their marriage he became a professor of English at Amherst College, where he stayed until 1875, when he was made the first president of Smith College. Mrs. Holland was always devoted to this younger couple, and the intimacy with them continued after the Hollands had moved to New York and the Seelyes to Northampton. Every visit to them gave her an additional opportunity to see the Dickinsons.

It is tempting to draw on the allusions to Mrs. Holland's visits in Emily's letters and let our imaginations recreate the scene. It appears that the visitor was shared by the entire household from Mrs. Dickinson, who found Mrs. Holland "so social," to Irish Maggie in the kitchen, who deemed her "a mistress most to be desired." The Hollands had always been fond of Lavinia, whose quick wit and exuberant interest in human affairs made her an entertaining companion. Little Mrs. Holland, with her feeling for reality and her lightness of touch, bringing with her a taste of the larger world, yet belonging with an indissoluble tie to the New England scene, whose essence lived in the very being of them all, had some specific value for each of these disparate persons.

One can see Emily, a little in the background, yet spiritually the center of the whole group, watching with an artist's pleasure, sensitive to all the overtones of the conversation, saying little but contributing much to the collective enjoyment.

There were also moments of privacy, sometimes stolen, when Emily and her "Elder Sister" as she called Mrs. Holland, could speak of the things that touched them closely. As in all enduring friendships, they shared something that belonged to them alone and which need not be stated to be understood. Although their individual lives had led them along different paths, they met on the common ground of essential human experience. Each in her own way brought to her living a sense of what was basic, and so each in her own way was able to enhance in the other the sense of being alive. The release of spirit, based on the assurance of being understood, which Emily felt in her first acquaintance with the Hollands, was continued throughout their lives.

"Life is the finest secret," Emily wrote in 1870, when she had already closed the doors to the outside world. Living deeply and sensitively behind the brick walls of her home, she found there infinitely more of life than most people glimpse in the crowded ways of society. In her letters to the Hollands, who lived in an ever widening circle of men and women, Emily Dickinson is seen not as a recluse, substituting abstraction for experience, but in all the warmth and color of an ardent human being, a consummate lover of life.

PART ONE

1853–1860

A traveler from Springfield to Amherst in the early 1850's covered the eighteen miles to Northampton by train, and thence was conveyed by stage over a covered bridge across the Connecticut and through the wide meadows that surround the village of Hadley, to the gently sloping rise on which Amherst stands. If he were the fortunate owner of good horses, he could drive all the way on the somewhat shorter carriage road in scarcely longer time. In the spring of 1853 Amherst celebrated its more direct connection with the larger centers by the opening of the Amherst and Belchertown Railway. This branch line intersected the road between Springfield and Boston at Palmer, where it connected with a north and south line already built from New London, Connecticut. On the ninth of June an excursion took place, which, according to the local paper, was for the purpose of introducing the citizens of New London to their neighbors at Amherst. Three hundred people came on a special train and were handsomely entertained by the Amherst citizens.

Emily Dickinson wrote an account of the event to her brother Austin, who was then studying law at Harvard. After describing the celebration, for which their father was chief marshal, she continued, "Dr. Holland was here, and called to see us – was very pleasant indeed, inquired for you, and asked Mother if Vinnie and I might come to see them in Springfield. . ." (*Letters*, p. 115).

Mr. and Mrs. Dickinson may have hesitated to accept the invitation for their daughters before they had become acquainted with the hostess, and they probably urged Dr. Holland to bring his wife to see them when he came again to Amherst. It was not long before he did so, for Emily wrote to her brother on the tenth of July:

> Dr Holland and his wife spent last Friday with us – came unexpectedly – we had a charming time, and have promised to visit them after Commencement. They asked all about you, and Dr

> Holland's wife expressed a great desire to see you. He said you would be a Judge — there was no help for it — you must certainly be a Judge! We had Champagne for dinner and a very fine time. We were sorry you were not here, and Dr and Mrs Holland expressed their regret many times. (*Emily Dickinson's Home,* Letters of Edward Dickinson and His Family, with comment and documentation by Millicent Todd Bingham, scheduled for publication by Harper & Brothers in 1951.)

Emily's references to Mrs. Holland as "Dr Holland's wife" make it clear that she was a new acquaintance, and the gala atmosphere of the occasion made an auspicious opening for the development of the friendship. With parental approval now assured, the girls accepted the invitation and made the visit in September, New England's favorite visiting season. In Letter V, written in September 1854, we find Emily referring to a day and night she had spent with the Hollands just a year before. Unfortunately no letter has been preserved that gives an account of this first visit, but the one to which I have given first place may have been written later that autumn, for its exuberance suggests the state of elation that comes in the early stages of a new friendship. "Minnie," whose name Emily added to those of Dr. and Mrs. Holland as if it were an afterthought dictated by courtesy to a person less known, was Mrs. Holland's sister Amelia, who lived with them until her marriage in 1856.

I

[Autumn 1853?]

Tuesday Evening.

Dear Dr. and Mrs. Holland, — dear Minnie — it is cold to-night, but the thought of you so warm, that I sit by it as a fireside, and am never cold any more. I love to write to you — it gives my heart a holiday and sets the bells to ringing. If prayers had any answers to them, you were all here to-night, but I seek and I don't find, and knock and it is not opened. Wonder if God is just — presume He is, however, and 'twas only a blunder of Matthew's.

I think mine is the case, where when they ask an egg, they get a scorpion, for I keep wishing for you, keep shutting up my eyes and looking toward the sky, asking with all my might for you, and yet you do not come. I wrote to you last week, but thought you would laugh at me, and call me sentimental, so I kept my lofty letter for "Adolphus Hawkins, Esq."

If it wasn't for broad daylight, and cooking-stoves, and roosters, I'm afraid you would have occasion to smile at my letters often, but so sure as "this mortal" essays immortality, a crow from a neighboring farm-yard dissipates the illusion, and I am here again.

And what I mean is this — that I thought of you all last week, until the world grew rounder than it sometimes is, and I broke several dishes.

Monday, I solemnly resolved I would be *sensible,* so I wore thick shoes, and thought of Dr. Humphrey, and the Moral Law. One glimpse of *The Republican* makes me break things again — I read in it every night.

Who writes those funny accidents, where railroads meet each other unexpectedly, and gentlemen in factories get their heads cut off quite informally? The author, too, relates them in such a sprightly way, that they are quite attractive. Vinnie was disappointed to-night, that there were not more accidents — I read the news aloud, while Vinnie was sewing. *The Republican* seems to us like a letter from you, and we break the seal and read it eagerly. . . .

Vinnie and I talked of you as we sewed, this afternoon. I said – "how far they seem from us," but Vinnie answered me "only a little way." . . . I'd love to be a bird or bee, that whether hum or sing, still might be near you.

Heaven is large – is it not? Life is short too, isn't it? Then when one is done, is there not another, and – and – then if God is willing, we are neighbors then. Vinnie and mother send their love. Mine too is here. My letter as a bee, goes laden. Please love us and remember us. Please write us very soon, and tell us how you are. . . .

Affectionately,

Emilie.

Emily's reading of the daily paper – a habit that persisted to the end of her life – was now given a highly personal interest by her direct association of the *Springfield Republican* with the Hollands. A cryptic little message which she sent as a New Year's greeting can only be interpreted in the light of her interest in Dr. Holland's work. On the second of January 1854 there appeared in the *Republican* the first chapter of Dr. Holland's first book, a *History of Western Massachusetts*. The *History* ran serially in weekly installments throughout that year and well into the next, and was published in book form in 1855. An announcement on the editorial page of the issue of January second calls it "a valuable attraction," adding, "Every son, daughter and cousin of this region, wherever now located, will want to possess that." Dr. Holland had probably been working on the book at the time of Emily's visit, and she took characteristic pleasure in her friend's achievement.

II

[2 January 1854]

January 2d.

May it come *today*?

Then New Year the sweetest, and long life the merriest, and the Heaven highest – by and by!

Emilie.

In the same mood of delight in a new friendship that characterized the first letter, Emily wrote again later in the winter. The discrepancy between her allusion to several nights passed at the Hollands' house the previous September and the implication in a later letter (V) that the visit consisted of only one day and night gives the impression that this letter might have been written a year later, following her second visit. Such inaccuracies are not uncommon in Emily's letters, however, and it is not the mood alone that places this one in its present position. Emily inquired for little Annie, the Hollands' only child at the time she had been with them, but not for the new baby Kate, born in November, whom she had not seen. She spoke also of Dr. Holland's presence at the time of the Cattle Show in October, which she could not have done the following year, when for reasons that will appear later Dr. Holland was detained at home.

The Annual Exhibition of the Hampshire Agricultural Society, popularly known as the "Cattle Show," drew visitors from all the neighboring towns, and was reported in the newspapers. Dr. Holland himself sometimes acted as reporter for the *Springfield Republican,* perhaps because he enjoyed the atmosphere of the occasion that turned the town into an enlarged family party, as well as for the opportunity it gave him to see the Dickinsons. There was a procession, a program with addresses, usually a public dinner to honor the speakers, and of course the usual exhibits and side shows of the typical county fair. Edward Dickinson always held a position of importance in the proceedings, and Mrs. Dickinson, Austin, and Lavinia took their turns as members of the various committees. In the autumn of 1853, the time Emily recalls in this letter, the Cattle Show was held on the twenty-sixth of October. Exercises were held in the College chapel, beginning with prayer by President Hitchcock and ending with an address by the Reverend F. D. Huntington of Boston, a native of Belchertown and a close friend of the Dickinson family, who was later to become the well known Bishop of Central New York. The carnival aspect of the fair is shown in Dr. Holland's account of his journey as it appeared in the newspaper report.

> I came from Palmer this morning by the extra freight and passenger train. We had for freight one moose, two buffaloes, and one fat woman. The passengers consisted of two soap professors, half a dozen of their professional brethren, and eight or ten private gentlemen.

It is improbable that Emily, who already disliked to mingle with crowds, attended the Cattle Show, but at that time she was still conforming to the pattern of village life by going to church. We cannot tell with certainty how long she continued to do so, for no direct references to her presence at the services appear in her published letters after 1854. When she no longer went to church, she still shared with her family the personal friendship of the ministers of the parish. At the time when this letter was written, the Reverend and Mrs. Edward S. Dwight were recent and very welcome arrivals at the First Congregational Church, to which the Dickinsons belonged, and became their warm friends. Mr. Dwight's preaching was the expression of a more liberal point of view than that of the typical small town preachers of the day, but occasionally an exchange of pulpits brought to the Amherst congregation reverberations from the thunder of Hell. It was after listening to such a sermon from a visiting clergyman that Emily sat down to comfort her spirit by writing to the Hollands.

III

[Early 1854?]

Sabbath Afternoon.

Dear Friends, — I thought I would write again. I write you many letters with pens which are not seen. Do you receive them?

I think of you all today, and dreamed of you last night.

When father rapped on my door to wake me this morning, I was walking with you in the most wonderful garden, and helping you pick — roses, and though we gathered with all our might, the basket was never full. And so all day I pray that I may walk with you, and gather roses again, and as night draws on, it pleases me, and I count impatiently the hours 'tween me and the darkness, and the dream of you and the roses, and the basket never full.

God grant the basket fill not, till, with hands purer and whiter, we gather flowers of gold in baskets made of pearl; higher — higher! It seems long since we heard from you — long, since how little Annie was, or any one of you — so long since Cattle Show, when Dr. Holland was with us. Oh, it always seems a long while from our seeing you, and even when at your house, the nights seemed much more long than they're wont to do, because separated from you. I want so much to know if the friends are all well in that dear cot in Springfield — and if well whether happy, and happy — *how* happy, and why, and what bestows the joy? And then those other questions, asked again and again, whose answers are so sweet, do they love — remember us — wish sometimes we were there? Ah, friends — dear friends — perhaps my queries tire you, but I so long to know.

The minister to-day, not our own minister, preached about death and judgment, and what would become of those, meaning Austin and me, who behaved improperly – and somehow the sermon scared me, and father and Vinnie looked very solemn as if the whole was true, and I would not for worlds have them know that it troubled me, but I longed to come to you, and tell you all about it, and learn how to be better. He preached such an awful sermon though, that I didn't much think I should ever see you again until the Judgment Day, and then you would not speak to me, according to his story. The subject of perdition seemed to please him, somehow. It seems very solemn to me. I'll tell you all about it, when I see you again.

I wonder what you are doing today – if you have been to meeting? Today has been a fair day, very still and blue. Tonight the crimson children are playing in the west, and tomorrow will be colder. How sweet if I could see you, and talk of all these things! Please write us very soon. The days with you last September seem a great way off, and to meet you again, delightful. I'm sure it won't be long before we sit together.

Then will I not repine, knowing that bird of mine, though flown – learneth beyond the sea, melody new for me, and will return.

Affectionately,

Emily.

In *Letters of Emily Dickinson* it is stated that the following poem was enclosed with the foregoing letter, but since both manuscripts are missing, I am not able to tell by comparison of the handwriting whether the two were written at the same time.

Truth is as old as God,
His twin identity –
And will endure as long as He,
A co-eternity,
And perish on the day
That He is borne away
From mansion of the universe,
A lifeless Deity.

The following spring Emily traveled to Washington with her sister Lavinia to join Mr. Dickinson, who was then serving as a member of Congress. It was the longest journey she ever made. The Washington *Daily Evening Star* for the seventh of April 1854 lists E. Dickinson and family from Massachusetts as recent arrivals at Willard's. Among other guests at the famous hotel while the Dickinsons were there was Ole Bull, the Norwegian violinist, but we have no record to show that Emily heard him play. It seems probable, however, that Edward Dickinson would have taken the girls to hear Henry Ward Beecher, who preached in Washington the ninth of April.

Five weeks from the day they left home, Emily wrote to Mrs. Holland from Philadelphia, where she and Lavinia were visiting the family of a cousin of their mother's, Mrs. Coleman, whose husband, the Reverend Lyman Coleman, had been principal of Amherst Academy while Emily was a pupil. While they lived at Amherst their daughters had been close friends of the Dickinson girls.

Circumstances point to this visit in Philadelphia as the time when Emily first met the Reverend Charles Wadsworth, then pastor of the Arch Street Presbyterian Church, of which the Coleman family were members. During the previous year the religious conflict with which Emily had been struggling since she was fifteen had been made more acute by the death of her friend Ben Newton. It is to be assumed that she now turned for aid to this man whose preaching touched the secret places of her spirit as no other's had done. In the twenty-eight years from their first meeting until his death Emily saw Dr. Wadsworth only on the few occasions when he called on her in Amherst, but ample evidence is given later in these letters to Mrs. Holland that she corresponded with him during much of that time. In 1862 he left Philadelphia for San Francisco, where he was pastor of Calvary Church until 1869, when he returned to Philadelphia to remain the rest of his life. The progress of Emily's friendship with the eminent clergyman – a friendship to which in later life she gave supreme value – can only be inferred from the letters she wrote after his death nearly thirty years later to his friend Mr. James D. Clark. In one of these she spoke of their relationship as "an intimacy of many years" (*Letters,* p. 344).

IV

[Mid-May 1854]

Philadelphia.

Dear Mrs. Holland and Minnie, and Dr. Holland too – I have stolen away from company to write a note to you; and to say that I love you still.

I am not at home – I have been away just five weeks today, and shall not go quite yet back to Massachusetts. Vinnie is with me here, and we have wandered together into many new ways.

We were three weeks in Washington, while father was there, and have been two in Philadelphia. We have had many pleasant times, and seen much that is fair, and heard much that is wonderful – many sweet ladies and noble gentlemen have taken us by the hand and smiled upon us pleasantly – and the sun shines brighter for our way thus far.

I will not tell you what I saw – the elegance, the grandeur; you will not care to know the value of the diamonds my Lord and Lady wore, but if you haven't been to the sweet

Mount Vernon, then I *will* tell you how on one soft spring day we glided down the Potomac in a painted boat, and jumped upon the shore – how hand in hand we stole along up a tangled pathway till we reached the tomb of General George Washington, how we paused beside it, and no one spoke a word, then hand in hand, walked on again, not less wise or sad for that marble story; how we went within the door – raised the latch he lifted when he last went home – thank the Ones in Light that he's since passed in through a brighter wicket! Oh, I could spend a long day, if it did not weary you, telling of Mount Vernon – and I will sometime if we live and meet again, and God grant we shall!

I wonder if you have all forgotten us, we have stayed away so long. I hope you haven't – I tried to write so hard before I went from home, but the moments were so busy, and then they *flew* so. I was sure when days *did* come in which I was less busy, I should seek your forgiveness, and it did not occur to me that you might not forgive me. Am I too late today? Even if you are angry, I shall keep praying you, till from very weariness, you will take me in. It seems to me many a day since we were in Springfield, and Minnie and the *dumb-bells* seem as vague – as vague; and sometimes I wonder if I ever dreamed – then if I'm dreaming now, then if I *always* dreamed, and there is not a world, and not these darling friends, for whom I would not count my life too great a sacrifice. Thank God there is a world, and that the friends we love dwell forever and ever in a house above. I fear I grow incongruous, but to meet my friends does delight me so that I quite forget time and sense and so forth.

Now my precious friends, if you won't forget me until I

get home, and become more sensible, I will write again, and more properly. Why didn't I ask before, if you were well and happy?

Forgetful

Emilie.

When September came around again the Hollands proposed another visit. The invitation came with their thanks for a gift of grapes and figs from the family at Amherst. It may be assumed that both fruits were the product of the Dickinsons' own garden, for Madame Bianchi speaks in *Emily Dickinson Face to Face* of her grandmother's fig trees, and there is other evidence that the Dickinsons went even beyond the usual high standard of the self-sustaining homes of the time in raising luxuries for their table. To raise grapes was quite usual, and they, like many others, made their own wine. But one hears with surprise of home-grown figs in New England until a study of the records of the Massachusetts Horticultural Society reveals that they were much more commonly grown in those days than in later times, when commercial cultivation in a climate more suited to them made the effort seem unprofitable.

Emily's note of acceptance was written only four days in advance of the date set for the visit. Her mother, who according to several of Emily's letters seemed inclined to illness when anything upset the family routine, had kept them for some days in suspense because she had not been well, but we have every reason to suppose the plan was carried through.

V

[September 1854]

Friday Evening.

Thank you, dear Mrs. Holland – Vinnie and I will come, if you would like to have us. We should have written before, but mother has not been well, and we hardly knew whether we could leave her, but she is better now, and I write quite late this evening, that if you still desire it, Vinnie and I will come. Then, dear Mrs. Holland, if agreeable to you, we will take the Amherst train on Tuesday morning, for Springfield, and be with you at noon.

The cars leave here at nine o'clock, and I think reach Springfield at twelve. I can think just how we dined with you a year ago from now, and it makes my heart beat faster to think perhaps we'll see you so little while from now.

To live a thousand years would not make me forget the day and night we spent there, and while I write the words, I don't believe I'm coming, so sweet it seems to me. I hope we shall not tire you; with all your other cares, we fear we should not come, but you *will* not let us trouble you, will you, dear Mrs. Holland?

Father and mother ask a very warm remembrance to yourself and Dr. Holland.

We were happy the grapes and figs seemed acceptable to you, and wished there were many more. I am very sorry to hear that "Kate" has such excellent lungs. With all your other cares, it must be quite a trial to you.

It is also a source of pleasure to me that Annie goes to sleep, on account of the "interregnum" it must afford to you.

Three days and we are there – happy – very happy! Tomorrow I will sew, but I shall think of you, and Sunday sing and pray – yet I shall not forget you, and Monday's very near, and here's to me on Tuesday! Good-night, dear Mrs. Holland – I see I'm getting wild – you will forgive me all, and not *forget* me all, though? Vinnie is fast asleep, or her love would be here — though she is, it is. Once more, if it is fair, we will come on Tuesday, and you love to have us, but if not convenient, please surely tell us so.

Affectionately,

Emilie.

Little Kate's first summer had left her in delicate health, and her tendency to cry, which Mrs. Holland had mentioned in her letter of invitation to Emily and Lavinia, was not a necessary exercise of the lungs as Emily suggested, but a sign of malnutrition. After the visit her condition became alarming, and in their anxiety her parents failed to write to their young friends at Amherst. Emily felt sadly cut off from them until a long-delayed note from Dr. Holland telling of the child's recovery was joyfully received. The Hollands had reason to be deeply thankful that her life had been spared, for as Emily's answering letter indicates, there had been many deaths among little children that year from cholera infantum and dysentery.

Dr. Holland's note also brought the news that he and his family were planning to move. Since their return to Springfield in 1849, they had been living in Mrs. Holland's old family home on Water Street near the river. The "Buff Cottage" which Dr. Holland bought in the autumn of 1854 stood on high ground which he thought would be more healthful for his children. It remained their home for eight years.

VI

[November 1854]

Saturday Eve.

I come in flakes, dear Dr. Holland, for verily it snows, and as descending swans, here a pinion and there a pinion, and anon a plume, come the bright inhabitants of the white home.

I know they fall in Springfield; perhaps you see them now — and therefore I look out again, to see if you are looking.

How pleasant it seemed to hear your voice — so said Vinnie and I, as we as individuals, and then collectively, read your brief note. Why didn't you speak to us before? We thought you had forgotten us — we concluded that one of the bright things had gone forever more. That is a sober feeling, and it mustn't come too often in such a world as this. A violet came up next day, and blossomed in our garden, and were it not for these same flakes, I would go in the dark and get it, so to send to you. Thank Him who is in Heaven, Katie Holland lives! Kiss her on every cheek for me — I really can't remember how many the bairn has — and give my warmest recollection to Mrs. Holland and Minnie, whom to love, this Saturday night, is no trifling thing. I'm very happy that you are happy — and that you cheat the angels of another one.

I would the many households clad in dark attire had succeeded so. You must all be happy and strong and well. I love to have the lamps shine on your evening table. I love to have the sun shine on your daily walks.

The "new house!" God bless it! You will leave the "maiden and married life of Mary Powell" behind.

Love and remember

Emilie.

In Emily's childhood her father had sold the family mansion to Deacon David Mack, and the Dickinsons had moved into a house on North Pleasant Street. After the deacon's death in 1854, Edward Dickinson bought the old house back. The *Hampshire and Franklin Express* for the twentieth of April 1855 congratulated him on repossessing it, but more than half a year passed before the family moved in. Mrs. Holland came to see them during the summer, and was probably shown the house in the course of renovation. The work must have suffered delays, for it seems to have been nearly Christmas time when the Dickinsons moved. Hearing nothing from Emily, Mrs. Holland wrote about the middle of January 1856 to inquire whether the move was safely accomplished, mentioning in her letter the death of her sister Sarah's husband, Otis Knight, on the twelfth of that month. Emily's reply gives the story of the "transit" from the old house to the new as if it had occurred so recently that its dislocating effect still lingered.

VII

[20? January 1856]

Sabbath Day.

Your voice is sweet, dear Mrs. Holland – I wish I heard it oftener.

One of the mortal musics Jupiter denies, and when indeed its gentle measures fall upon my ear, I stop the birds to listen. Perhaps you think I *have* no bird, and this is rhetoric – pray, Mr. Whately, what is *that* upon the cherry-tree? Church is done, and the winds blow, and Vinnie is in that pallid land the simple call "sleep." They will be wiser by and by, we shall all be wiser! While I sit in the snows, the summer day on which you came and the bees and the south wind, seem fabulous as *Heaven* seems to a sinful world – and I keep remembering it till it assumes a *spectral* air, and nods and winks at me, and then all of you turn to phantoms and vanish slow away. We cannot talk and laugh more, in the parlor where we met, but we learned to love for aye, there, so it is just as well.

We shall sit in a parlor "not made with hands" unless we are very careful!

I cannot tell you how we moved. I had rather not remember. I believe my "effects" were brought in a band-box, and the "deathless me," on foot, not many moments after. I took at the time a memorandum of my several senses, and also of my hat and coat, and my best shoes – but it was lost in the *mêlée,* and I am out with lanterns, looking for myself.

Such wits as I reserved, are so badly shattered that repair is useless – and still I can't help laughing at my own catastrophe. I supposed we were going to make a "transit," as heavenly bodies did – but we came budget by budget, as our fellows do, till we fulfilled the pantomime contained in the word "moved." It is a kind of *gone-to-Kansas* feeling, and if I sat in a long wagon, with my family tied behind, I should suppose without doubt I was a party of emigrants! They say that "home is where the heart is." I think it is where the *house* is, and the adjacent buildings.

But, my dear Mrs. Holland, I have another story, and lay my laughter all away, so that I can sigh. Mother has been an invalid since we came *home,* and Vinnie and I "regulated," and Vinnie and I "got settled," and still we keep our father's house, and mother lies upon the lounge, or sits in her easy chair. I don't know what her sickness is, for I am but a simple child, and frightened at myself. I often wish I was a grass, or a toddling daisy, whom all these problems of the dust might not terrify – and should my own machinery get slightly out of gear, *please,* kind ladies and gentlemen, some one stop the wheel, – for I know that with belts and bands of gold, I shall whizz triumphant on the new stream! Love for you – love for Dr. Holland – thanks for his exquisite hymn – tears for your sister in sable, and kisses for Minnie and the bairns.

From your mad

Emilie.

In the course of the next three years Emily probably wrote a number of letters to Mrs. Holland that have not been preserved. The one that follows may have been chosen for special safe keeping because it is so full of the ecstasy of living that made Emily seem equally at home in this world and the next. Since her expression still retains some of its youthful effusiveness, and there are no allusions to fix the time of writing, the date under which it was first published still seems appropriate. The departure of the bobolinks, which she noted in a postscript, sets the season at about the first of August, the time when those cheerful birds disappear from the shorn meadows. If the year was 1856, the letter would have been written a month after an event which marked an important change in Emily's family life, for on the first of July Austin Dickinson had married her close friend Susan Gilbert. Their father built a house for the young couple next door, and the solid family group in the brick mansion broke ranks to take in a new member. Happy as she was in the acquisition of a new sister, Emily had been so intimate with each of the partners that it could not have been altogether easy for her to accept the exclusive nature of their new relation, but in this letter, which may have been written soon after the wedding, no hint of such a difficulty appears.

VIII

[Early August 1856?]

Sabbath Night.

Don't tell, dear Mrs. Holland, but wicked as I am, I read my Bible sometimes, and in it as I read today, I found a verse like this, where friends should "go no more out;" and there were "no tears," and I wished as I sat down to-night that we were *there* – not *here* – and that wonderful world had commenced, which makes such promises, and rather than to write you, I were by your side, and the "hundred and forty and four thousand" were chatting pleasantly, yet not disturbing us. And I'm half tempted to take my seat in that Paradise of which the good man writes, and begin forever and ever *now*, so wondrous does it seem. My only sketch, profile, of Heaven is a large, blue sky, bluer and larger than the *biggest* I have seen in June, and in it are my friends – all of them – every one of them – those who are with me now, and those who were "parted" as we walked, and "snatched up to Heaven."

If roses had not faded, and frosts had never come, and one had not fallen here and there whom I could not waken, there were no need of other Heaven than the one below – and if God had been here this summer, and seen the things that *I* have seen – I guess that He would think His Paradise superfluous. Don't tell Him, for the world, though, for after all He's said about it, I should like to see what He *was* building for us, with no hammer, and no stone, and no journeyman either. Dear Mrs. Holland, I love, to-night – love you and Dr. Holland, and "time and sense" – and fading things, and things that do *not* fade.

I'm so glad you are not a blossom, for those in my garden fade, and then a "reaper whose name is Death" has come to get a few to help him make a bouquet for himself, so I'm glad you are not a rose – and I'm glad you are not a bee, for where they go when summer's done, only the thyme knows, and even were you a robin, when the west winds came, you would coolly wink at me, and away, some morning!

As "little Mrs. Holland," then, I think I love you most, and trust that tiny lady will dwell below while we dwell, and when with many a wonder we seek the new Land, *her* wistful face, *with* ours, shall look the last upon the hills, and first upon – well, *Home!*

Pardon my sanity, Mrs. Holland, in a world *insane*, and

love me if you will, for I had rather *be* loved than to be called a king in earth, or a lord in Heaven.

Thank you for your sweet note — the clergy are very well. Will bring such fragments from them as shall seem me good. I kiss my paper here for you and Dr. Holland — would it were cheeks instead.

Dearly,

Emilie.

P.S. The bobolinks have gone.

There is an interval of more than two years between the midsummer letter we have just read and the next, written in autumn mood. These two years are more obscure for us than any other time in Emily's adult life, for there are no published letters to other friends that fill in the gap. The latest letters to her former schoolmates that have been printed are dated 1853, and her correspondence with Mr. and Mrs. Bowles did not begin until 1858. Her letters to her cousins Louisa and Frances Norcross began in 1859, and those to Thomas Wentworth Higginson in 1862.

We may assume that her friendship with the Hollands continued to grow, and that letters and even visits were exchanged, but when she wrote the November letter some time had elapsed since they had met. The letter is dated for us by an allusion to the death from scarlet fever of a little girl, the daughter of Dick, the Dickinsons' stableman. Although Dick is not given a family name in any of Emily's letters, he is mentioned in two of those to the Misses Norcross (*Letters,* pp. 219, 230). In the second, written in 1863, we are told that Dick had a large family, and that one little girl had died. Another letter (p. 217) tells of a little boy named Sammie Matthews, without mentioning his parents. Since the Amherst death records show that on the first of November 1858 a little girl of eight named Harriet, the daughter of Richard and Ann Matthews, died of scarlet fever, there seems to be no doubt that the child is the one of whom Emily writes. Ever sensitive to the inroads of death, her vision of an ultimate heaven is dimmed by the fear of immediate loss, but how real the fear is to her at the moment of writing is hard to guess from the playfulness with which she treats the subject.

IX

[November 1858]

Saturday Eve.

Dear Hollands, – Good-night! I can't stay any longer in a world of death. Austin is ill of fever. I buried my garden last week – our man, Dick, lost a little girl through the scarlet fever. I thought perhaps that *you* were dead, and not knowing the sexton's address, interrogate the daisies. Ah! dainty – dainty Death! Ah! democratic Death! Grasping the proudest zinnia from my purple garden, – then deep to his bosom calling the serf's child!

Say, is he everywhere? Where shall I hide my things? Who is alive? The woods are dead. Is Mrs. H. alive? Annie and Katie – are they below, or received to nowhere?

I shall not tell how short time is, for I was told by lips which sealed as soon as it was said, and the open revere the shut. You were not here in summer. *Summer*? My memory flutters – had I – was there a summer? You should have seen the fields go – gay little entomology! Swift little ornithology! Dancer, and floor, and cadence quite gathered away, and I a phantom, to you a phantom, rehearse the story! An orator of feather unto an audience of fuzz, – and pantomimic plaudits. "Quite as good as a play," indeed!

Tell Mrs. Holland she is mine. Ask her if *vice versa*? Mine is but just the thief's request – "Remember me to-day." Such are the bright chirographies of the "Lamb's Book." Good-night! My ships are in! – My window overlooks the wharf! One yacht, and a man-of-war; two brigs and a schooner! "Down with the topmast! Lay her a' hold, a' hold!"

Emilie.

In March 1859 Lavinia went to Boston for a prolonged visit with her mother's younger sister, Mrs. Loring Norcross, who was in poor health and needed her cheery companionship, since her own two daughters were still school girls. Emily conceded this occasional borrowing of her sister with considerable inner resistance, but accepted it as inevitable. While Lavinia was gone, Susan Dickinson had as a guest an old school friend, Kate Scott, who later became Mrs. Anthon. Emily, who had not met her before, found her a charming companion who added to the gaiety of the evenings she spent with the young people next door. On one of these occasions her dislike of meeting strangers led her into an embarrassing situation. The two men who were the cause of the incident were the Honorable Reuben A. Chapman, a leading citizen of Springfield, and William Hyde, a lawyer of Ware. Judge Chapman, at one time Chief Justice of the Supreme Court of Massachusetts, was the founder of "The Club," a small group of prominent Springfield men, including Dr. Holland, who met for supper one evening each week.

These two men had been called to Amherst the previous June to arbitrate a dispute of long standing between two factions of the South Congregational Church of Amherst, and were obliged to make several trips continuing through the winter before a settlement could be reached. On the twenty-second of March they concluded the affair by advising one faction to sue the other for recovery of their property, a decision that must have done little to heal the breach. On their numerous visits over this dispute, they had probably been often at Edward Dickinson's house, where on neutral ground their standing would have been purely social, and Emily must have been well acquainted with them. Had she known who they were when they rang the doorbell she would not have run away, but in her letter she states plainly that it was already her custom to run from strangers.

X

[Late March 1859]

Not alone to thank you for your sweet note, is my errand, dear Mrs. Holland, though I do indeed, but will you please to help me?

I guess I have done wrong, I don't know certainly, but Austin tells me so, and he is older than I, and knows more of ordinances.

When Vinnie is here, I ask her; if she says I sin, I say, "Father, I have sinned." If she sanctions me, I am not afraid, but Vinnie is gone now, and to my sweet elder sister, in the younger's absence, something guides my feet.

These are the circumstances. Your friend and neighbor, Mr. Chapman, was in town last week, with Mr. Hyde of Ware, as a business ally. They called upon us Wednesday evening, and were our guests on the evening following. After most pleasant conversations, we parted for the night, the gentlemen then proposing to return next day. Business did not terminate, and sitting next evening with ——, as I often do, some one rang the bell and I ran, as is my custom.

What was my surprise and shame, on hearing Mr. Chapman ask for "*Mrs*. D!" K.S., a guest of ——'s, was my confederate, and clinging fast like culprit mice, we opened consultation. Since the dead might have heard us scamper, we could not allege that we did not run, besides, it was *untrue,* which to people so scared as we, was a minor consideration, but would have its weight with our seniors. I proposed that we ask forgiveness.

K. was impenitent and demurred. While we were yet deliberating, —— opened the door, announced that we were detected, and invited us in.

Overwhelmed with disgrace, I gasped a brief apology, but the gentlemen simply looked at us with grave surprise.

After they had retired, Austin said we were very rude, and I crept to my little room, quite chagrined and wretched. Now do you think Mr. Chapman will forgive me? I do not mind Mr. Hyde of Ware, because he does not please me, but Mr. Chapman is my friend, talks of my books with me, and I would not wound him.

I write a little note to him, saying I am sorry, and will he forgive me, and remember it no more?

Now will I ask so much of you, that you read it for me, judge if it is said as yourself would say it, were *you* rude instead of me – that if you approve, when you walk again, you will take it for me to Mr. Chapman's office, tell him for me, intercede as my sister should? Then if he forgives me, I shall write you quickly, but if he should not, and we meet the next in Newgate, know that I was a loving felon, sentenced for a door bell.

Emilie.

Mrs. Holland's days were fully occupied with the care of her family, and she could not respond to letters as often or as promptly as Emily wished. When she failed to answer, Emily was sometimes tempted to doubt her affection, as is shown in this letter, probably written in the summer of 1859. If that date is correct, the fact that Mrs. Holland was expecting her third child would account for the rumor that had reached Emily's ears that she was not in good health. The obscure allusion to Herod may be explained in the light of this coming event, assuming that Emily knew of it and that her association with the name had to do with the king who sought to destroy the Christ-child. If she had not heard the news she might have used the name of Herod as a general term for a tyrant – in this case a sly thrust at Mrs. Holland's husband, whose devotion was coupled with a dependence that made constant demands on her. Since it was to both husband and wife that she addressed her letter, she might have hoped that the tyrant himself would write to her, even though her only open request was for a reply without words from eight-year-old Annie.

XI

[Summer 1859?]

Friday

Dear Friends, – I write to you. I receive no letter.

I say "they dignify my trust." I do not disbelieve. I go again. *Cardinals* wouldn't do it. Cockneys wouldn't do it, but I can't *stop* to strut, in a world where bells toll. I hear through visitor in town, that "Mrs. Holland is not strong." The little peacock in me, tells me not to inquire again. Then I remember my tiny friend – how brief she is – how dear she is, and the peacock quite dies away. Now, you need not speak, for perhaps you are weary, and "Herod" requires all your thought, but if you are *well* – let Annie draw me a little picture of an erect flower; if you are *ill*, she can hang the flower a little on one side!

Then, I shall understand, and you need not stop to write me a letter. Perhaps you laugh at me! Perhaps the whole United States are laughing at me too! *I* can't stop for that! *My* business is to love. I found a bird, this morning, down – down – on a little bush at the foot of the garden, and wherefore sing, I said, since nobody *hears*?

One sob in the throat, one flutter of bosom – "*My* business is to *sing*" — and away she rose! How do I know but cherubim, once, themselves, as patient, listened, and applauded her unnoticed hymn?

Emily.

One day during the summer of 1859 Emily and Lavinia caught a tantalizing glimpse of the Hollands on their way to some unknown destination. This meeting could hardly have occurred at Amherst unless they were traveling by carriage, for the Amherst and Belchertown Railway would not have carried them beyond that town, but if they had been driving they could have stopped long enough to tell their friends where they were going. It seems more likely that the girls themselves were taking a trip to Northampton and saw them for a few hurried moments as their train passed through the railway station.

Emily's questions in this letter regarding the Hollands' home life show that while she had not visited them for some time, she had been with them at a date later than the last visit mentioned in these letters and was well acquainted with the house in which they were then living. In any case, the Hollands' visits to Amherst were far more frequent, and Emily's anticipation of seeing them there in September suggests that their coming was an annual event to be expected at summer's close. If they disappointed her in 1859 we know that they came the following year, for the names of Dr. and Mrs. Holland, their two little girls, and Lavinia Dickinson appear on the register of the Amherst College Museum for the twentieth of September 1860.

The approach of autumn never failed to bring Emily a sense of the insecurity of life. In September 1859 her feeling was made more acute by the knowledge that her aunt Mrs. Norcross was incurably ill and was not expected to live until Christmas. On a cold and lonely evening she turned to the Hollands, begging for a word from them. This is the last letter she addressed jointly to husband and wife, for her friendship with Mrs. Holland was becoming more personal, and it was not long after this that she began to call her "Sister." Already she had asked her to act the part of sister in her request for help the previous March (Letter X). When Mrs. Holland, whose life was filled with happy relationships, read the passage in this September letter beginning "Sisters are brittle things," she must have found it touching, and in her reply she may have suggested that Emily adopt her as a second sister.

XII

[September 1859]

Dear Hollands, — Belong to me! We have no fires yet, and the evenings grow cold. To-morrow, stoves are set. How many barefoot shiver I trust their Father knows who saw not fit to give them shoes.

Vinnie is sick to-night, which gives the world a russet tinge, usually so red. It is only a headache, but when the head aches next to you, it becomes important. When she is well, time leaps. When she is ill, he lags, or stops entirely.

Sisters are brittle things. God was penurious with me, which makes me shrewd with Him.

One is a dainty sum! One bird, one cage, one flight; one song in those far woods, as yet suspected by faith only!

This is September, and you were coming in September. Come! Our parting is too long. There has been frost enough. We must have summer now, and "whole legions" of daisies.

The gentian is a greedy flower, and overtakes us all. Indeed, this world is short, and I wish, until I tremble, to touch the ones I love before the hills are red — are gray — are white — are "born again"! If we knew how deep the crocus lay, we never should let her go. Still, crocuses stud many mounds whose gardeners till in anguish some tiny, vanished bulb.

We saw you that Saturday afternoon, but heedlessly forgot

to ask where you were going, so did not know, and could not write. Vinnie saw Minnie flying by, one afternoon at Palmer. She supposed you were all there on your way from the sea, and untied her fancy! To say that her fancy wheedled her is superfluous.

We talk of you together, then diverge on life, then hide in you again, as a safe fold. Don't leave us long, dear friends! You know we're children still, and children fear the dark.

Are you well at home? Do you work now? Has it altered much since I was there? Are the children women, and the women thinking it will soon be afternoon? We will help each other bear our unique burdens.

Is Minnie with you now? Take her our love, if she is. Do her eyes grieve her now? Tell her she may have half ours.

Mother's favorite sister is sick, and mother will have to bid her good-night. It brings mists to us all; – the aunt whom Vinnie visits, with whom she spent, I fear, her last inland Christmas. Does God take care of those at sea? My aunt is such a timid woman!

Will you write to us? I bring you all their loves – *many*.

They tire me.

Emilie.

In the autumn Dr. Holland started on one of the lecture tours that occupied much of his time during the winter months from 1858 to 1868. He was in great demand on the "Lyceum" circuits, not only in the east, but reaching out into the rapidly developing middle west as far as Iowa and Nebraska. Everywhere on his tours he met large audiences who came to hear him speak on such subjects as "Work and Play," "Conflict," and "American Social Life." Mingled with his interest in the human contacts and the rewarding pleasure of work sincerely done, he always felt an aching homesickness as he traveled interminably — and often with great discomfort — up and down the country from one small town to another. His longing for home must have been intensified almost beyond endurance when he received a telegram from Springfield dated the seventh of December 1859, telling him that he had a son. The *Springfield Republican* of the same day brought the news in a brief announcement to the friends at Amherst, and Emily sat down at once to write to the baby's mother.

XIII

[8? December 1859]

God bless you, dear Mrs. Holland! I read it in the paper.

I'm so glad it's a little boy, since now the little sisters have some one to draw them on the sled — and if a grand old lady you should live to be, there's something sweet, they say, in a son's arm.

I pray for the tenants of that holy chamber, the wrestler, and the wrestled for. I pray for distant father's heart, swollen, happy heart!

Saviour keep them all!

Emily.

Mrs. Holland seems to have answered Emily's note as soon as she was able, probably addressing her letter to both the sisters, for shortly afterwards she received a letter from Lavinia. Since only two of Lavinia's letters to Mrs. Holland have been preserved, it has seemed worth while to include them in this book in order that her personality may speak for itself. By her lifelong devotion she made it possible for Emily to live according to her own inner needs, yet she herself was as strongly individual as her more gifted elder sister.

XIV

[December 1859]

Home.

My Dear Mrs. Holland

I'm so glad you are safe & I know you are happy. I hope you did not pass through very "deep waters."

I suppose it's a comfort to meet one's own selection!

I wish I could look in upon your new joy. I fancy your husband is somewhat impatient to see "mother & child." I had it in my heart to write sooner but I feared you could not attend to foreign documents.

Your letter was sweet, Mrs. Holland & I thank you for writing when you were really ill.

You must not be ill very long.

We shall love to hear how you are when any body can tell us. I always keep you in remembrance. Love to your Mother & husband & kisses for the children.

Mother sends love & was surprised when the daily press opened her innocent eyes!

Good night, dear Mrs. Holland, God keep you safely.

Very sincerely

Vinnie

The following brief note, first printed without a date, was placed next to one that has now been dated 1865 (Letter XIX), but the signature *Emilie* marks it as having been written no later than 1861, when Emily abandoned that spelling. She sent many such little notes to her friends, often using the third person in referring to them, as she sometimes did in speaking of herself. It is possible that this one came to Mrs. Holland with a flower from Emily's small conservatory after the birth of the little boy.

XV

[December 1859?]

Will someone lay this little flower on Mrs. Holland's pillow?

Emilie.

In spite of the fears of her family, Mrs. Dickinson's sister, Mrs. Norcross, survived the winter, but Lavinia was again summoned before spring came and remained with her aunt until she died on the seventeenth of April 1860. Without her sister's presence, Emily felt ill equipped for the exigencies to be met in any contact with the outside world. While she was alone something occurred that made her turn again to her "elder sister" for help. We have no clue by which to discover the circumstances, for Emily's request seems to have involved inquiries concerning some person whom she chose not to name. Mrs. Holland complied, and the next letter brought Emily's thanks.

It is tempting to try to place this mysterious letter after the one in which Emily told of her embarrassment at having run away from Judge Chapman and Mr. Hyde the year before and to suppose that Mrs. Holland had taken Emily's apologies to Mr. Chapman and reported that he had received them with complacency. Lavinia had been away at that time also, but other circumstances mentioned in this letter do not fit the earlier date. Emily had just read in the *Springfield Republican* that Dr. Holland was about to return home after a long absence. In March 1859 he was not away, but on the seventeenth of March 1860 the paper contained the following item:

> Dr. Holland of this city concluded at Belchertown last evening a season of ninety lectures, involving constant travel through a period of four months and a half. Within a period of sixteen months he has traveled nearly 20,000 miles, and delivered 156 lectures and public addresses.

XVI

[March 1860]

Wednesday.

"Sister."

You did my will. I thank you for it. Let me work for you! What prettier negotiation than of friend for friend? I did not suspect complacency in "Mr Brown of Sheffield"! It is plain that Vinnie is gone – she assays them for me.

Complacency! My Father! in such a world as this, when we must all stand barefoot before thy jasper doors!

Thank you for putting me on trail. I will make quite a fox, in time, unless I die early.

I gather from "Republican" that you are about to doff your weeds for a Bride's Attire. Vive le fireside! Am told that fasting gives to food marvellous Aroma, but by birth a Bachelor, disavow Cuisine.

Meeting is well worth parting. How kind in some to die, adding *impatience* to the rapture of our thought of Heaven!

As by the dead we love to sit —
Become so wondrous dear —
As for the lost we grapple
Though all the rest are here —
In broken Mathematics
We estimate our prize
Vast, in it's *fading* ratio
To our penurious eyes.

I had rather you lived nearer — I would like to touch you. Pointed attentions from the Angels, to two or three I love, make me sadly jealous.

People with *Wings* at option, look loftily at hands and feet, which induces watchfulness! How gay to love one's friends! How *passing* gay to fancy that they reciprocate the whim, tho' by the Seas divided, tho' by a single Daisy hidden from our eyes! I would not exchange it for all the funds of the Father. Vinnie is yet in Boston. Thank you for recollecting. I am somewhat afraid at night, but the Ghosts have been very attentive, and I have no cause to complain. Of course one cant expect one's furniture to sit still all night, and if the Chairs do prance – and the Lounge polka a little, and the shovel give it's arm to the tongs, one dont mind such things! From fearing them at first, I've grown to quite admire them, and now we understand each other, it is most enlivening! How near, and yet how far we are! The new March winds could bring me, and yet "whole legions of Angels" may lie between our lips!

Emilie

The Hollands' baby, who was named Theodore, was operated on when less than a year old to correct a congenital trouble with the tendons of one foot. He gained the use of his foot, but walked with a limp during his childhood. His lameness called forth a special tenderness from his father, who wrote to him about 1865, "I would give all my old boots to have you in my arms. How is that dear little foot? Love me, darling, and write again." Sensitively aware of the parents' feelings in passing through this ordeal, Emily wrote to express her sympathy and to inquire how the baby was getting on.

XVII

[1860]

How is your little Byron? Hope he gains his foot without losing his genius. Have heard it ably argued that the poet's genius lay in his foot — as the bee's prong and his song are concomitant. Are you stronger than these? To assault so minute a creature seems to me malign, unworthy of Nature — but the frost is no respecter of persons.

I should be glad to be with you, or to open your letter. Blossoms belong to the bee, if needs be by *habeas corpus*.

Emily.

In handwriting similar to that of Letter XVI came this little poem in the latter half of the 1850 decade. A rosebud, tied by a narrow green ribbon through slits in the notepaper on which it is written, gives the explanation. Emily discovered it in some sheltered corner and shared her pleasure with Mrs. Holland. A garden-minded reader is left in doubt, however, about the season, for New Englanders will know that the little rosebud that bloomed out of time is likely to have appeared in the warm days of Indian summer, yet Emily suggests that it led the way to the advance of spring. Tied to a poem, it could, perhaps, do so at any season.

Baffled for just a day or two —
  Embarrassed — not afraid —
Encounter in my garden
  An unexpected maid!
She beckons, and the woods start —
  She nods, and all begin —
Surely such a country
  I was never in!

Emilie

PART TWO

1865–1868

From the period between 1860 and 1865 no letters remain. No single reason has been found to account for the gap, but aside from the fact that the interval covered the years of the Civil War, a time of tension and anxiety for all Americans, several occurrences in the lives of the correspondents may also have been responsible.

There are indications that during those years critical changes were taking place in Emily's inner life. It was then she first made open acknowledgment that she was a poet by writing for criticism to Thomas Wentworth Higginson, after reading his article "To a Young Contributor" in the *Atlantic Monthly* of April 1862. In one of her first letters to him she threw light on her reason for seeking his help, confiding that she had experienced an emotional crisis which she described as "a terror since September, I could tell to none" (*Letters,* p. 273). She took the artist's path to redemption, and in her poems found her way through the dark maze of her distress. It has been supposed by several writers that the crisis that overtook her in 1861 was related to an emotional involvement with Dr. Wadsworth, but it seems more in keeping with the trend of her life to assume that whatever the complications in her personal relations, they were only the outward manifestations of a deep psychic disturbance marking the transition from a youthful phase to one more mature. In that case Dr. Wadsworth's role would have been that of the rock to which a shipwrecked person clings, and his departure in the spring of 1862 for distant San Francisco would have forced her back upon her own inner resources to fight her secret battle.

She did not cease to write letters; indeed she started an active correspondence with Mr. Higginson, and the published letters of about this time to Samuel Bowles and his wife show special warmth and intensity of feeling. Perhaps she found these newer friends more important to her during the period of her emotional stress; her letters to Mrs. Holland may have been less frequent, yet there was certainly no break in the friendship. It is possible that those she did write were lost or destroyed when the Hollands moved again in 1862.

By that time Dr. Holland had become prosperous enough to build a large house on a finely wooded site overlooking the Connecticut River, two miles north of the center of Springfield. The family became greatly attached to the place, which they named Brightwood, and though they lived there only ten years, it was the home that held the richest associations for the children as they looked back upon it in after years. The house remained identified with the Hollands in the minds of the community for a long time, and later provided the name for the section of the city that grew up around it.

In 1864 the correspondence between Emily and Mrs. Holland may have been seriously interrupted when Emily developed trouble with her eyes. She spent two long periods of exile in the course of that year and the next in a Cambridge boardinghouse, where she lived with her cousins Louisa and Frances Norcross while under the care of a Boston physician. The use of her pen was forbidden while her eyes were under treatment, and she wrote few but the most necessary letters. We know, however, that she was working on her poems, for she wrote to Colonel Higginson, "I work in my prison, and make guests for myself" (*Letters*, p. 280). A little poem that came to Mrs. Holland in handwriting which was said by Mrs. Todd to be of this period was probably sent as a brief message in place of a letter, and seems to have been written in a homesick mood soon after her arrival in Cambridge.

> Away from home are some and I,
> An emigrant to be
> In a metropolis of homes
> Is common possibility.*
>
> The habit of a foreign sky
> We difficult acquire,
> As children who remain in face,
> The more their feet retire.

*Alternative line: *Is easy, possibly.*

When we pick up the thread of connection between the friends again, in the autumn of 1865 after Emily had returned to Amherst, we find that relations were still close and that news was being exchanged. A few days before this letter was written, Emily's sister-in-law, Susan Dickinson, had gone to Geneva, New York, to be with her sister Martha Gilbert Smith, whose little girl of two years had died on the third of November. The Smiths had no other child, having lost a baby boy four years earlier, and Emily, who was very fond of Mrs. Smith, found her sympathy strongly aroused. Madame Bianchi records a little poem she wrote at the time and sent to Susan Dickinson for whom the child was named (*Emily Dickinson Face to Face*, p. 253).

Another recent event — one which more immediately affected Emily's life — was the marriage of the Dickinsons' servant, Margaret, and her consequent departure. Although Emily gives only the first name of the bride and the last name of the groom, the marriage was presumably the one recorded at St. Jerome's parish in Holyoke between Margaret O'Bryan and Stephen Lawler on the eighteenth of October 1865. In those days there was no Catholic church in Amherst or Northampton, and although Mass was occasionally said in the homes of the parishioners, wedding ceremonies were performed at the church in the rapidly developing industrial center down the river. Since the groom had been married before, but not the bride, Emily's phrase "vicarious papa to four previous babes" is somewhat confusing, and gives point to her remark at the beginning of the letter about the difficulty of telling the truth.

XVIII

[Early November 1865]

Dear Sister, — Father called to say that our steel-yard was fraudulent, exceeding by an ounce the rates of honest men. He had been selling oats. I cannot stop smiling, though it is hours since, that even our steel-yard will not tell the truth.

Besides wiping the dishes for Margaret, I wash them now,

while she becomes Mrs. Lawler, vicarious papa to four previous babes. Must she not be an adequate bride?

I winced at her loss, because I was in the habit of her and even a new rolling-pin has an embarrassing element, but to all except anguish, the mind soon adjusts.

It is also November. The noons are more laconic and the sundowns sterner, and Gibraltar lights make the village foreign. November always seemed to me the Norway of the year. ——— is still with the sister who put her child in an ice nest last Monday forenoon. The redoubtable God! I notice where Death has been introduced, he frequently calls, making it desirable to forestall his advances.

It is hard to be told by the papers that a friend is failing, not even know where the water lies. Incidentally, only, that he comes to land. Is there no voice for these? Where is Love today?

Tell the dear Doctor we mention him with a foreign accent, party already to transactions spacious and untold. Nor have we omitted to breathe shorter for our little sister. Sharper than dying is the death for the dying's sake.

News of these would comfort, when convenient or possible.

Emily.

Several allusions in the letter we have just read are open to conjecture. Emily's inquiry for a friend who was "failing" has as yet no trustworthy explanation. Assuming that the word "failing" has to do with the health of the friend referred to, the rest of the passage appears so figurative that its meaning is obscure. It is possible that an error occurred in the original transcription or the printing of the 1894 edition, but as the manuscript is missing, there is no way to prove whether this reading is correct. If instead of the word "failing" one should read "sailing," the allusion might be more literal than it now appears. Samuel Bowles had recently taken a trip to California, returning by sea. His letters "Across the Continent" were published after his return, and were currently appearing in the *Springfield Republican.* The installment of the twenty-eighth of October was written in San Francisco the day before sailing, but did not mention for what port he was bound. Meanwhile, the paper had announced his return by way of Panama and New York.

Another recent event in the lives of Emily's friends was the publication in October 1865 of Dr. Holland's *Life of Abraham Lincoln.* The following year a German translation of the book was brought out by the same publishers in Springfield. It was probably in connection with the plans for this edition in a foreign language that Emily imagined "transactions spacious and untold" in which Dr. Holland might soon be involved.

The final sentences of the letter imply that Mrs. Holland was at that time deeply concerned over the imminent death of a friend. That the person was unknown to Emily is suggested by the fact that she expressed anxiety for Mrs. Holland herself rather than for the one who was ill. The same feeling is carried over to the letter that follows, which seems to indicate that Mrs. Holland had been gravely affected by the death of her friend. It is with this sequence in mind that I have placed the letter next, though it is possible to give a different interpretation to the phrase, "the house which had lost its friend." Judging by the meaning Emily put into the word "friend" in later letters, we might infer that she was alluding here to Dr. Holland, who was away on one of his prolonged lecture tours. In a letter to Colonel Higginson, written in 1875, she spoke of his wife as "your friend," and in a late letter of this series she referred to Annie Holland's husband as "Annie's friend." The poem with which the letter closes, however, is more appropriate if read in the light of the first interpretation. There might have been some personal allusion in the passage that was deleted for publication in 1894, which would have made the meaning clear.

XIX

[Late 1865?]

Dear Sister, — It was incredibly sweet that Austin had seen you, and had stood in the dear house which had lost its friend. To see one who had seen you was a strange assurance. It helped dispel the fear that you departed too, for notwithstanding the loved notes and the lovely gift, there lurked a dread that you had gone or would seek to go. "Where the treasure is," there is the prospective.

Austin spoke very warmly and strongly of you, and we all felt firmer, and drew a vocal portrait of Kate at Vinnie's request, so vivid that we saw her. . . .

> Not all die early, dying young,
> Maturity of fate
> Is consummated equally
> In ages or a night.
> A hoary boy I've known to drop
> Whole-statured, by the side
> Of junior of fourscore — 't was act,
> Not period, that died.

We can almost hear the sap beginning to run when we read the letter Emily wrote the following March — the month that excited and stimulated her more than any other. As a whole, however, the letter is tantalizing because of the fragmentary character given it by the deletions made when it was first published.

At the first sign of spring she was already looking forward to seeing the Hollands in the coming summer, when they would be at Amherst for commencement. Her "Cousin Peter," from whom she learned that they would be in town for the occasion, was Perez Cowan from Knoxville, Tennessee, who was to graduate in the class of 1866. Amherst College commencement was an important event of the year in the Connecticut Valley, drawing speakers and guests from the larger world. A recognized part of the celebration was the reception at the home of the treasurer, Edward Dickinson, and for some years after Emily had withdrawn from general society, she still saw the guests who came to "Papa's fête."

XX

[March 1866]

. . . February passed like a skate and I know March. Here is the "light" the stranger said "was not on sea or land." Myself could arrest it, but will not chagrin him.

. . . Cousin Peter told me the Doctor would address Commencement — trusting it insure you both for papa's fete I endowed Peter.

We do not always know the source of the smile that flows to us. . . .

My flowers are near and foreign, and I have but to cross the floor to stand in the Spice Isles.

The wind blows gay today and the jays bark like blue terriers.

I tell you what I see — the landscape of the spirit requires a lung, but no tongue. I hold you few I love, till my heart is red as February and purple as March.

Hand for the Doctor.

Emily.

Mrs. Holland did not wait until commencement time to visit Amherst, but came in the early spring, bringing with her a bunch of trailing arbutus, the spring's first flowers. Early in May Emily wrote her a letter which we can date by two widely contrasting events mentioned in it. The first of these, the death of a young woman whom Emily did not name, was recorded in the *Hampshire Express* of the third of May 1866 as follows, "In this town, May 1, Mrs. Laura, wife of Frank W. Dickey of Marshal, Michigan, and youngest daughter of L. M. Hills, Esq. of this town, aged 27 years." The fact that Mr. Hills' land lay next to the Dickinsons' on the east explains Emily's phrase "at the end of our garden."

The second event was a circus procession which passed the house when the "Colossal Travelling Exhibition of G. T. Bailey & Co." visited Amherst on Friday, May third. The Dickinsons' house lay on the route from the railroad station to the center of town through which the circus passed on its way to the north end of the village, where its tents were set up in advance. The announcement stated that there would be a gigantic Hippopotamus (asserted by many to be identical with the Behemoth of Holy Writ), Elephants, and a Comprehensive Menagerie, as well as equestrian and gymnastic exhibitions, and that there would be nothing in the performances to offend the most cultivated, moral, or refined.

XXI

[Early May 1866]

Dear Sister, — After you went, a low wind warbled through the house like a spacious bird, making it high but lonely. When you had gone the love came. I supposed it would. The supper of the heart is when the guest is gone.

Shame is so intrinsic in a strong affection we must all experience Adam's reticence. I suppose the street that the lover travels is thenceforth divine, incapable of turnpike aims.

That you be with me annuls fear and I await Commencement with merry resignation. Smaller than David you clothe me with extreme Goliath.

Friday I tasted life. It was a vast morsel. A circus passed the house – still I feel the red in my mind though the drums are out.

The book you mention, I have not met. Thank you for tenderness.

The lawn is full of south and the odors tangle, and I hear today for the first the river in the tree.

You mentioned spring's delaying – I blamed her for the opposite. I would eat evanescence slowly.

Vinnie is deeply afflicted in the death of her dappled cat, though I convince her it is immortal which assists her some. Mother resumes lettuce, involving my transgression – suggestive of yourself, however, which endears disgrace.

"House" is being "cleaned." I prefer pestilence. That is more classic and less fell.

Yours was my first arbutus. It was a rosy boast.

I will send you the first witch hazel.

A woman died last week, young and in hope but a little while – at the end of our garden. I thought since of the power of death, not upon affection, but its mortal signal. It is to us the Nile.

You refer to the unpermitted delight to be with those we love. I suppose that to be the license not granted of God.

Count not that far that can be had,
Though sunset lie between –
Nor that adjacent, that beside,
Is further than the sun.

Love for your embodiment of it.

Emily.

The Hollands probably carried out their plan to be present at the Amherst College commencement, but there is no record of an address by Dr. Holland in the program. According to an announcement of coming events in the *Hampshire Express* of the fifth of July 1866, he was to read a poem as part of the program of the Phi Beta Kappa Society. When the commencement events were reported in the next week's issue, there was no mention of the poem, and no copy of the Phi Beta Kappa program has been obtainable.

While in Amherst the Hollands almost certainly stayed with the Seelyes, and it may have been after this visit that they received the following note from Lavinia, which implies that they had not been staying with the Dickinsons but had been "prisoners" of someone else.

XXII

[About 1866]

Dear Friends

I'm lonely since you went away, kind o' ship-wrecked like! Perhaps I miss you! You'll come again soon & *then* be *my* prisoners. You'll be a comfort & a shelter. Good night. God bless & keep you,

Vinnie

Mrs. Holland's fondness for Lavinia sometimes led her into the error of writing to the sisters together to save time, but she found that Emily's insistence on the highly individual nature of friendship made the practice unacceptable. After receiving Emily's emphatic rebuke in the following letter, she seems to have avoided this pitfall.

XXIII

[About 1867]

Sister, — A mutual plum is not a plum. I was too respectful to take the pulp and do not like a stone.

Send no union letters. The soul must go by Death alone, so, it must by life, if it is a soul.

If a committee — no matter.

I saw the sunrise on the Alps since I saw you. Travel why to Nature, when she dwells with us? Those who lift their hats shall see her, as devout do God.

I trust you are merry and sound. The chances are all against the dear, when we are not with them, though paws of principalities cannot affront if we are by.

Dr. Vaill called here Monday on his way to your house to get the Doctor to preach for him. Shall search *The Republican* for a brief of the sermon. Today is very homely and awkward as the homely are who have not mental beauty.

The sky is low, the clouds are mean,
A travelling flake of snow
Across a barn or through a rut
Debates if it will go.

A narrow wind complains all day
How someone treated him;
Nature, like us, is sometimes caught
Without her diadem.

Another poem that may have accompanied the gift of a rose from Emily's garden was written, according to Mrs. Todd, between 1862 and 1868. Since the loss of the manuscript makes it impossible to date it more exactly, it is added here to complete the group of letters and poems remaining from this decade.

Though my destiny be fustian
Hers be damask fine –
Though she wear a silver apron,
I, a less divine,

Still, my little gypsy being,
I would far prefer,
Still my little sunburnt bosom
To her rosier.

For when frosts their punctual fingers
On her forehead lay,
You and I and Dr. Holland
Bloom eternally,

Roses of a steadfast summer
In a steadfast land,
Where no autumn lifts her pencil,
And no reapers stand.

In May 1868 the Hollands found a tenant for their house, and following the custom of the time for those who could afford to do so, the whole family sailed for Europe, where they spent the next two years. Emily's frequent use of geographical names to evoke images had little to do with the realities to be met in travel, and the ocean seemed to her an almost insuperable barrier between her and her friends. When Samuel Bowles went to Europe in 1862 she wrote to him, "You sleep so far, how can I know you hear?" (*Letters*, p. 196). Whether it was because she did not try to reach Mrs. Holland while she was away, or because that practical lady kept her correspondence tidied up as she went, to the loss of later generations, it is the unfortunate fact that no letters from those years have been preserved.

The Hollands made the usual tour by slow stages, visiting Great Britain, France, Switzerland, Germany, and Italy, making long stops in centers where each one, according to age and capacity, could absorb something of the culture of the country. Dr. Holland himself studied French and German, and wrote to his friend and publisher Charles Scribner, "It is worth twenty years of work to roam over these old fields of art and civilization." The family joined the American colony in Rome for a few months, but unlike many of his compatriots, Dr. Holland was not able to throw off his Puritanism sufficiently to fall under the spell of the ancient capital, where the domination of the Vatican was distasteful to him. The best medical advice was sought for Mrs. Holland, who had been suffering from serious trouble with her eyes, and she was treated by an eminent oculist in Berlin, only to learn that she must expect diminished sight for the rest of her life. Little Theodore fared better, for while he was at school at Geneva the trouble with his foot was corrected by a Swiss specialist and his walking became entirely normal.

During this interlude abroad Dr. Holland was forming plans for the work he wished to do when he returned to America. Before he left home, Charles Scribner had asked him to take over the direction of the magazine *Hours at Home,* and the offer had remained open to him. He had come to believe, however, that there was a field for a new magazine that would cover more aspects of the life of the day and reach a wider circle of readers than the literary periodicals then in existence, and he did not care to tie himself to any connections that would limit his freedom to develop such a project. While he was considering how his plan could be carried out, an American friend who shared his views came to Europe with his family and joined the Hollands in Switzerland. Roswell C. Smith, a lawyer from Indiana, was a man in whose character and business judgment Dr. Holland had great confidence. As a result of their consultations, the two men decided to unite forces in trying to establish a magazine of broad scope and high literary standards, which should be, as Dr. Holland wrote to his friend later, "an aggressive, free speaking thing, with a flavor of vitality about it." Leaving Paris on the eve of the outbreak of war with Germany early in May 1870, the Holland family turned their faces eagerly toward home.

PART THREE

1870–1874

After their two years in Europe, the Hollands were very happy to return to Brightwood and American ways of living. Dr. Holland turned all his energies into the enterprise he had planned while abroad — the launching of the new magazine, *Scribner's Monthly*. A company was formed which functioned separately, but was associated with Charles Scribner and Company, and the magazine absorbed *Hours at Home* and two other periodicals.

According to Robert Underwood Johnson, who was later a member of his staff, Dr. Holland and his business partner, Roswell Smith, aimed at nothing less than leadership in political, religious, artistic, and social opinion. Although this goal was somewhat too high for realization, the magazine was successful from the start. In addition to the wide range of subjects it covered, it introduced several features in form and content that had an influence on the character of other American magazines. *Scribner's Monthly* first used photography in the process of engraving, making possible a freer use of illustrations. The articles followed current trends in thought, from new discoveries in science to the "higher criticism" of the Bible, and Dr. Holland's editorials on "Topics of the Time" dealt simply and often forcefully with many phases of contemporary life. With the taste of his young associate, Richard Watson Gilder, to support him, Dr. Holland introduced several new writers of fiction, such as George W. Cable and Frances Hodgson Burnett, while among his other contributors appeared many of the best known names of the day, both American and English.

Of course the Dickinsons were among the first subscribers to *Scribner's Monthly*, and in her letters Emily sometimes commented on the stories or articles she read in it.

In late September or early October 1870, Mrs. Holland called unexpectedly on the Dickinsons. Since Emily's letter, referring to this visit, is more concerned with an incident of the call than with the fact that she had seen her friend again, it seems probable that this was not the first time they had been together since the Hollands' return from Europe. Colonel Higginson, writing to his wife about his first visit to his "scholar" in Amherst, the seventeenth of August 1870, enclosed a picture of Mrs. Browning's tomb as a gift from Emily, who had received it from Dr. Holland. Although it might have been sent in a letter from Europe, it is more likely that it was among the large collection of photographs that Dr. Holland brought home, and that he gave it to her after his return.

During Mrs. Holland's call, Emily seems to have spoken of a note she would soon send her, apparently to be delivered to someone else. Fearing that something in her manner might have given her friend a false impression, she wrote soon after to disclaim any intentions of intrigue, and to explain that on further reflection she had decided not to send the note after all.

Dr. Holland's work kept him much in New York during October, when the first issue of the magazine was being prepared for the press. The girls were also away from home, at Miss Porter's School at Farmington, Connecticut. It is characteristic of Emily that she should have thought of Mrs. Holland's loneliness in terms of her inability to use her eyes, for it had been the custom for someone in the family to read aloud to her. Mr. Chapman, to whom Emily jokingly refers as a possible substitute for Dr. Holland as a reader, has already been introduced in Letter X. Mr. Buckingham, another candidate, was pastor of the South Church in Springfield, and a member of "The Club" which Mr. Chapman had founded.

While apples were falling in Amherst, Paris was being besieged by the Germans, but Emily found Bismarck less important than "ourselves."

XXIV

[October 1870]

I guess I wont send that note now, for the mind is such a new place, last night feels obsolete.

Perhaps you thought, dear Sister, I wanted to elope with you and feared a vicious Father.

It was not quite that.

The Papers thought the Doctor was mostly in New York. Who then would read for you? Mr Chapman, doubtless, or Mr Buckingham! The Doctor's sweet reply makes me infamous.

Life is the finest secret.

So long as that remains, we must all whisper.

With that sublime exception I had no clandestineness.

It was lovely to see you and I hope it may happen again. These beloved accidents must become more frequent.

We are by September and yet my flowers are bold as June. Amherst has gone to Eden.

To shut our eyes is Travel.

The Seasons understand this.

How lonesome to be an Article! I mean – to have no soul.

An Apple fell in the night and a Wagon stopped.

I suppose the Wagon ate the Apple and resumed it's way.

How fine it is to talk.

What Miracles the news is!

Not Bismark but ourselves.

The Life we have is very great.
The Life that we shall see
Surpasses it, we know, because
It is Infinity.
But when all Space has been beheld
And all Dominion shown
The smallest Human Heart's extent
Reduces it to none.

Love for the Doctor, and the Girls.
Ted might not acknowledge me.

Emily.

Emily's hesitation about sending the note mentioned in the last letter may have taken a positive turn again a few-days later, for the little penciled message that follows, in the handwriting of this period though written on a scrap of paper of an earlier date, was sent with an enclosure which seems to have been a letter of sympathy to be conveyed by Mrs. Holland to a third person. In her previous letter, Emily had given as her reason for not sending the note a change in her own feeling about it, but this time the delay, which would bring the letter to its destination after the occasion was past, is attributed to Lavinia, who had some share in carrying out the plan.

XXV

[October 1870?]

Our little Note was written several days ago, but delayed for Vinnie. Perhaps it's circumstances cease. Tears do not outgrow, however, so I venture sending.

Landscapes reverence the Frost, though it's gripe be past.

It was not many months before Emily and Mrs. Holland met again. An undated letter from Mrs. Holland to Kate at boarding school, which appears to have been written in the spring of 1871, tells of her visiting the Seelyes at Amherst and, though she did not mention the Dickinsons, there is no doubt that she took the opportunity to see them.

A letter that Emily must have written soon after this visit implies that Mrs. Holland had brought her a box of candy and had carried her sewing with her when she called on the Dickinsons, leaving her thimble behind when she went home. It had been Emily's hope to see her friend alone before she left, perhaps in the passage which was her favorite place for private interviews, but privacy was hard to obtain in the Dickinson house and her maneuvers had failed. After her return, Mrs. Holland seems to have written to inquire for the thimble and to have received the following reply.

XXVI

[Spring 1871]

I have a fear I did not thank you for the thoughtful Candy.

Could you conscientiously dispel it by saying that I did?

Generous little Sister!

I will protect the Thimble till it reaches Home —

Even the Thimble has it's Nest!

The Parting I tried to smuggle resulted in quite a Mob at last! The Fence is the only Sanctuary. That no one invades because no one suspects it.

Why the Thief ingredient accompanies all Sweetness Darwin does not tell us.

Each expiring Secret leaves an Heir, distracting still.

Our unfinished interview like the Cloth of Dreams, cheapens other fabrics.

That Possession fairest lies that is least possest.

Transport's mighty price is no more than he is worth —

Would we sell him for it? That is all his Test.

Dont affront the Eyes —

Little Despots govern worst.

Vinnie leaves me Monday — Spare me your remembrance while I buffet Life and Time without —

Emily.

The thimble must have been of little use to Mrs. Holland after it was returned, for later that year her eyes gave her serious trouble. Finding that the disease from which she suffered was progressing, the oculist forbade her to read or write. She probably dictated the letter which Emily now answers, to warn her friend that it might be some time before she would hear from her again. Emily enters a plea for the continued use of an amanuensis, using the steam engine as an example of how power may be controlled and conveyed. Since the current happenings of her world often provided the occasion for her figures of speech, it is not surprising to learn that one of the newly-appointed railroad commissioners of Massachusetts was a man who would have been known to both the Holland and Dickinson families. Albert D. Briggs of Springfield, whose appointment was made on the twenty-second of November 1871, was a member of "The Club" to which Dr. Holland belonged, and a close friend of Samuel Bowles. Emily's father, who was greatly concerned with the development of the railroads in the state, had doubtless been interested in securing the appointment.

XXVII

[Late November 1871]

Dear Sister.

Bereavement to yourself your faith makes secondary. We who cannot hear your voice are chastened indeed –

"Whom he loveth, he punisheth," is a doubtful solace finding tart response in the lower Mind.

I shall cherish the Stripes though I regret that your latest Act must have been a Judicial one. It comforts the Criminal little to know that the Law expires with him.

Beg the Oculist to commute your Sentence that you may also commute mine. Doubtless he has no friend and to curtail Communion is all that remains to him.

This transitive malice will doubtless retire – offering you anew to us and ourselves to you.

I am pleased the Gingerbread triumphed.

Let me know your circumstance through some minor Creature, abler in Machinery if unknown to Love.

Steam has his Commissioner, tho' his substitute is not yet disclosed of God.

Emily.

There is no indication that Emily ever visited the Hollands after 1860, and it is known that she never left home after she returned from Cambridge for the second time in 1865. That her friends did not yet fully accept her withdrawal, however, is implied in the next letter, which is a refusal of an invitation to visit them.

Between the autumn of 1870 and the spring of 1872, Dr. Holland attempted to carry on his work in New York while continuing to make Springfield his home – a plan which kept him constantly coming and going. Annie left school before Christmas 1870 because of eyestrain, but was often with her father in New York or away on visits. In the autumn of 1871 Ted also went away to school, and Mrs. Holland must have found herself sometimes deserted. It may have been at a time when she expected to be alone that she wrote a letter urging Emily to break her habit of solitude and come to stay with her in Springfield.

XXVIII

[1872]

That so trifling a Creature grieve any I could hardly suppose – though with Love all things are possible.

Thanking you tenderly as a child for a sweet favor I can never go. This will not retard my place in Affection, will it?

I shall still be mentioned when the children come?

Some must seem a Traitor, not because it is, but it's Truth belie it.

André had not died had he lived today.

Only Love can wound –

Only Love assist the Wound.

Worthier let us be of this Ample Creature.

If my Crescent fail you, try me in the Moon.

This will make no difference in the daily dearness?

You will keep the same Face and myself no other Heart, with the slight repairs Thought and Nature make –

In adequate Music there is a Major and a Minor –

Should there not also be a Private?

Good Night – I am going to sleep if the Rat permit me – I hear him singing now to the tune of a Nut.

I could wish to know, be it by a trifle, that you name me still.

Emily.

When *Scribner's Monthly* became well established, Dr. Holland began to feel that he could no longer continue to live in so disjointed a fashion, trying to maintain his home in Springfield while carrying on his work in New York. In the spring of 1872 he bought a house on Park Avenue, in the Murray Hill section of New York, and the family came there to live the following autumn. Kate had finished school, and the Hollands were united again, except for Ted, who was at school at Washington, Connecticut. At first they hoped to keep Brightwood for a summer home, but the climate of Springfield did not give the family the refreshing change they needed, and the place was reluctantly sold the following year.

The period of moving and settling was a very difficult one for Mrs. Holland, whose eye disease had reached an acute stage. It became necessary to operate, and in the summer of 1872 one eye was removed. The ordeal was a severe one, but she came through it with her usual cheerfulness, and in spite of the dim sight of the remaining eye, she was thankful for relief from the pain she had so long suffered. Dr. Holland must have sent a report of the operation to the Dickinsons, for Emily wrote shortly after the event a letter which shows how well she understood her friend's attitude of simple acceptance.

XXIX

[August 1872]

To have lost an Enemy is an Event with all of us – almost more memorable perhaps than to find a friend. This severe success befalls our little Sister – and though the Tears insist at first, as in all good fortune, Gratitude grieves best.

Fortified by Love, a few have prevailed.

"Even so, Father, for so it seemed faithful in thy Sight."

We are proud of her safety – Ashamed of our dismay for her who knew no consternation.

It is the Meek that Valor wear too mighty for the Bold.

We should be glad to know of her present Lifetime, it's project, though a little changed – so precious to us all.

Be secure of this, that whatever waver – her Gibraltar's Heart is firm.

Emily.

Although Emily no longer left home, Lavinia had continued to visit the Hollands in Springfield. Now she traveled as far as New York to see them in their new house on Park Avenue, reporting her impressions with characteristic vividness to Emily on her return. Mrs. Holland had once declared that Lavinia could have more adventures in traveling from Amherst to Springfield than most people experience in a trip to Europe, so it may be imagined how inflated the little visit became by the time it reached Emily's ears. Emily took vicarious pleasure in her sister's happiness, and wrote to express her gratitude. The singular form of her statement about the closeness of the tie between her and her sister might lead us to infer that this letter was written after the death of their parents, but the reference to her father at the end shows that he was still with them.

It is probable that Lavinia's visit, which took place in the spring, was made in 1873, the first year in which the Hollands occupied their new house, for the following spring, the last before her father's death, she was very busy at home, as is shown in Letter XXXIII.

XXX

[Early summer 1873]

I was thinking of thanking you for the kindness to Vinnie.

She has no Father and Mother but me and I have no Parents but her.

She has been very happy and returns with her Sentiments at rest.

Enclosed please find my gratitude.

You remember the imperceptible has no external Face.

Vinnie says you are most illustrious and dwell in Paradise. I have never believed the latter to be a superhuman site.

Eden, always eligible, is peculiarly so this noon. It would please you to see how intimate the Meadows are with the Sun. Besides —

> The most triumphant Bird I ever knew or met
> Embarked upon a twig to-day
> And till Dominion set
> I famish to behold so eminent a sight

And sang for nothing scrutable
But intimate Delight.
Retired, and resumed his transitive Estate —
To what delicious Accident
Does finest Glory fit!

While the Clergyman tells Father and Vinnie that "this Corruptible shall put on Incorruption" – it has already done so and they go defrauded.

Emily –

The Hollands adapted themselves happily to life in the broader environment of New York. The ban on the theater had been lifted during their years in Europe, the girls attended dances, and Dr. Holland himself developed a taste for the music of Wagner, which was then just being introduced. Public recognition had already opened a place for him in the social life of the city, and invitations to evening receptions at his house were sent to a long list of people in the literary world and in various fields of public life. Though stronger drinks than tea or coffee were never served, the rooms were always crowded, and among those who became familiar guests were William Cullen Bryant, Henry M. Stanley, Bret Harte, and Henry Ward Beecher.

Adding to her other activities the role of hostess, Mrs. Holland's days became filled with absorbing occupations, and the correspondence probably suffered a lapse which was the occasion of the following inquiry from Emily, in the epigrammatic manner most characteristic of her writing in the early 1870's. It was written at a time when the severe financial panic of September 1873 left more than half the railroads in the United States in the hands of receivers. As she often did, Emily turned the news of the day into a figure of speech, using it to express her sense of loss in the long separation from her friend.

XXXI

[September? 1873]

Owning but little Stock in the "Gold of Ophir" I am not subject to large Reverses – though may not the small prove irreparable? I have lost a Sister. Her name was not Austin and it was not Vinnie. She was scant of stature though expansive spirited and last seen in November – Not the November heretofore, but Heretofore's Father.

Trite is that Affliction which is sanctified. "I have chosen whom I have chosen."

Possibly she perished?

Extinction is eligible.

Science will not trust us with another World.

Guess I and the Bible will move to some old fashioned spot where we'll feel at Home.

Emily.

Emily's appeal to her lost sister seems to have been effective, for there is proof in a letter written the following spring (XXXIII) that Mrs. Holland visited Amherst in the autumn of 1873. Since the letter that now follows mentions a recent meeting as if it had been a rare occurrence, it was probably written soon after that autumn visit. When she left, Mrs. Holland had taken with her a spray of flowers or a cutting from Emily's cape jasmine, one of her favorite plants that grew in the small conservatory opening from the dining-room. Since it was autumn, it was probably the cutting rather than the flowers which Emily, who understood the ways of plants, had given to her friend with directions about how to root it and raise a plant of her own.

XXXII

[Autumn 1873]

Little Sister.

I miss your childlike Voice –

I miss your Heroism.

I feel that I lose combinedly a Soldier and a Bird.

I trust that you experience a trifling destitution.

Thank you for having been.

These timid Elixirs are obtained too seldom.

Thank you for every Patience. You won the love of all, even a sweet remark from Austin, in itself an achievement.

I am glad "the Jessamine lived."

To live is Endowment. It puts me in mind of that singular Verse in the Revelations – "Every several Gate was of one Pearl."

Little Sister – Good Night – I am sure you went.

Parting is one of the exactions of a Mortal Life. It is bleak – like Dying, but occurs more times.

To escape the former, some invite the last. The Giant in the Human Heart was never met outside.

The Sun came out when you were gone.

I chid him for delay –

He said we had not needed him. Oh prying Sun!

Love for Doctor.

Emily.

This poem is in writing closely similar to that of the preceding letter. Bearing Emily's signature, it may have been sent as a message by itself, or perhaps enclosed with a letter from which it has since become separated.

Longing is like the Seed
That wrestles in the Ground
Believing if it intercede
It shall at length be found.

The Hour and the Clime —
Each Circumstance unknown,
What Constancy must be achieved
Before it see the Sun!

Emily.

Edward Dickinson spent the winter and spring of 1874 in Boston as a member of the Massachusetts state legislature, representing the town of Amherst in the interests of a projected railway line, the Massachusetts General Railroad. He threw himself wholeheartedly into his public speeches, showing more fervor than he usually allowed himself in private conversation, and expressing himself clearly, forcefully, and sometimes wittily. Emily wrote to the Norcross sisters early in the year that her father was ill at home. She said, "I think it is the 'Legislature' reacting on an otherwise obliging constitution" (*Letters,* p. 250). He recovered sufficiently, however, to continue his efforts at Boston throughout the spring.

In May Emily wrote Mrs. Holland an account of the activities of the household during her father's absence. For the first time in these letters she mentioned the Irish servant Maggie Maher, with whom Mrs. Holland would already have been well acquainted, since she had been with the family for several years. She came into the Dickinson household in the late 1860's and remained with Emily and Lavinia for the rest of their lives. The robustness of her mind and body gave to her loyalty the quality of a somewhat awkward but faithful watchdog, and to the Dickinsons' friends she came to hold a place of her own in contributing to the vital atmosphere of the house.

XXXIII

[May 1874]

Little Sister.

I hope you are safe and distinguished. Is the latter the former? Experience makes me no reply.

Nature begins to work and I am assisting her a little, when I can be spared.

It is pleasant to work for so noble a Person.

Vinnie and "Pat" are abetting the Farm in Papa's absence. A Triumph of Schemes, if not of Executions. Pat is as abnegating as a Dromedary and I fear will find his Lot as unique.

When you were here – there were Flowers and there are Flowers now, but those were the Nosegays of Twilight and these – are the Nosegays of Dawn –

It is plain that some one has been asleep!

Suffer Rip – Van Winkle!

Vinnie says Maggie is "Cleaning House." I should not have suspected it, but the Bible directs that the "Left Hand" circumvent the Right!

We are to have another "Circus," and again the Procession from Algiers will pass the Chamber-Window.

The Minor Toys of the Year are alike, but the Major – are different.

But the dimensions of each subject admonish me to leave it.

Love, though, for your own. When a Child and fleeing from Sacrament I could hear the Clergyman saying "All who loved the Lord Jesus Christ – were asked to remain" –

My flight kept time to the Words.

Emily.

Written on a scrap of paper, these lines were tucked into one of the letters of about this time. Although Emily did not know that the spring of 1874 was the evening of her father's life, and that for her a new day was soon to begin, it seems appropriate to place the little poem at the end of this group of letters.

When Memory is full
Put on the perfect Lid –
This Morning's finest syllable
Presumptuous Evening said –

PART FOUR

1875–1881

The weather was hot in Boston on the sixteenth of June 1874, when Edward Dickinson addressed the Massachusetts legislature on the proposed Hoosac Tunnel, the building of which would greatly enhance the usefulness of the railroad in which he was interested. In the midst of his speech he felt faint and was obliged to sit down; then, becoming alarmed, he retired to his hotel room, where he called a physician while preparing to go home to Amherst. But he was too ill to make the journey, and before any of his family could reach him, he died after an illness of only a few hours.

The foundations of Emily's life were severely shaken. She wrote to her cousins (*Letters*, p. 255), "You might not remember me, dears. I cannot recall myself. I thought I was strongly built, but this stronger has undermined me." Though she was intellectually independent and spiritually unconfined by the limits of her environment, she found security for living in the inescapable absoluteness of her father's character. If his word was law in the affairs of the household, his firm will meant safety for those who lived under his authority. Yet his dominating influence could hardly be called despotic, for his power lay in self-discipline rather than in the exercise of moral coercion. Different as she was from her father in mind and temperament, it was from him that Emily derived much of her own strength of character. Each recognized the separateness of the other's strongly marked personality and made allowances for the difference. Whatever lightness Edward Dickinson permitted himself found a sensitive response in Emily, and a shy, unspoken tenderness had existed between them.

In a letter to Mrs. Holland seven months after the event, Emily wrote of his death as the cardinal fact in the current life of the family. The note of bitterness in her words, "His firm Light—quenched so causelessly," suggests that she found special anguish in the thought that if her father had remained at home, or if he had been attended by his own physician, his life would not have ended so soon or so abruptly. She never visited her father's grave, but Mrs. Holland, whose name was not in the papers as one of those attending the funeral, probably paid her last respects to Mr. Dickinson at a later time by a visit to the cemetery, from which she brought Emily a clover from his grave (see Letter XXXVI). A spray of clover, with several leaves and heads of bloom, which it is almost safe to assume to be the one that passed from Mrs. Holland's hand to Emily's, still lies pressed between the pages of her Bible, testifying its significance to her. The little friendly act made such an impression on Emily that she alluded to it in several later letters.

The rigors of winter make the loneliness more intense, as Emily now writes of the great change that has come into her home.

XXXIV

[Late January 1875]

Sister.

This austere Afternoon is more becoming to a Patriot than to one whose Friend is it's sole Land.

No event of Wind or Bird breaks the Spell of Steel.

Nature squanders Rigor – now – where she squandered Love.

Chastening – it may be – the Lass that she receiveth.

My House is a House of Snow – true – sadly – of few.

Mother is asleep in the Library – Vinnie – in the Dining Room – Father – in the Masked Bed – in the Marl House.

How soft his Prison is —
How sweet those sullen Bars —
No Despot — but the King of Down
Invented that Repose!

When I think of his firm Light – quenched so causelessly, it fritters the worth of much that shines. "Dust unto the

Dust" indeed – but the final clause of that marvelous sentence – who has rendered it?

"I say unto you," Father would read at Prayers, with a militant Accent that would startle one.

Forgive me if I linger on the first Mystery of the House.

It's specific Mystery – each Heart had before – but within this World. Father's was the first Act distinctly of the Spirit.

Austin's Family went to Geneva, and Austin lived with us four weeks. It seemed peculiar – pathetic – and Antediluvian. We missed him while he was with us and missed him when he was gone.

All is so very curious.

Thank you for that "New Year" – the first with a fracture. I trust it is whole and hale – to you.

"Kingsley" rejoins "Argemone" –

Thank you for the Affection. It helps me up the Stairs at Night, where as I passed my Father's Door – I used to think was safety. The Hand that plucked the Clover – I seek, and am

Emily.

The security in which Emily had lived until she was past forty had given her a certain detachment from the ordinary responsibilities of a mature person. For a year after Edward Dickinson's death, the family life was carried on in his memory, and Emily's experience of adjustment to her loss was one of the spirit rather than an outward adaptation to new circumstances. Just a year from the day he died, Mrs. Dickinson succumbed to a stroke of paralysis, bringing a startling change into the daily life of the household. The little mother who had quietly but adequately provided the background of daily living became a helpless invalid, and the roles of mother and daughter were reversed. At first Mrs. Dickinson was very ill, but later she made a gradual though only partial recovery. Three years later she fell and broke her hip and never was able to stand again. From the beginning of her illness in 1875 until she died in 1882, her daughters tended her, hoping at first that she would improve but gradually finding themselves with a helpless child on their hands.

How the word of this new trouble reached Mrs. Holland we do not know; possibly it was Lavinia who wrote to tell her of it, for no letter from Emily remains that gives an account of her mother's attack. Two short notes are all we now have to cover a period of a year and a half, from January 1875 to August 1876. Between the first and the second a definite change developed in her handwriting, and it seems probable that the first, thanking the Hollands for a book they had sent her, was written before the event that so seriously affected her life. Since this letter, though addressed to Mrs. Holland, includes her husband in its message of thanks, the gift may very well have been a volume of Dr. Holland's own work – possibly his novel *Sevenoaks,* which was published in 1875.

XXXV

[1875]

Sister –

I have the little Book and am twice triumphant — Once for itself, and once for Those who enabled me.

The embarrassment of the Psalmist who knew not what to render his friend – is peculiarly mine – Though he has canceled his consternations, while my own remain.

Thank you with all my strength – and Doctor as yourself – And again yourself for the sweet note.

Nature assigns the Sun —
That — is Astronomy.
Nature cannot enact a Friend —
That – is Astrology.

Emily.

Emily's days were filled with the practical duties involved in caring for her mother, but her private inner life was intensified. In her own room at night she worked on her poems, and answered Colonel Higginson when he inquired about her writing, "I have no other playmate" (*Letters*, p. 294). She sent him copies of some of her poems, among them one she called an "Epitaph," a copy of which she sent also to Mrs. Holland. On the upper corners of the notepaper on which it is written are pasted two little cuts from newspapers, one showing a star and crescent, the other a corner in an old graveyard, with tombstones leaning against one another. This poem, with two others which are also in the writing of about 1875, may have come to Mrs. Holland during the interval of about a year between the last letter and the next. Since each of the three poems is on a different kind of paper, Emily probably sent them one at a time. The first is the "Epitaph."

She laid her docile Crescent down
And this mechanic Stone
Still states to Dates that have forgot
The News that She is gone –

So constant to its stolid Trust
The Shaft that never knew,
It shames the Constancy that fled
Before its emblem flew.

Emily.

Summer laid her simple Hat
On its boundless Shelf
Unobserved – a Ribin slipt
Snatch it for Yourself.

Emily.

A little Madness in the Spring
Is wholesome even for the King,
But God be with the Clown –
Who ponders this tremendous scene –
This whole Experiment of Green –
As if it were his own!

Emily.

The little note that comes next contained an enclosure, and the wording implies that the request that accompanies it need not be expressed because it has been made so many times before. On the outside of the folded sheet Emily has written "Mrs. Holland," to distinguish it from the enclosed letter that is intended for someone else. It has always been understood by the Holland family that for many years Emily made a practice of sending to Mrs. Holland the letters she wrote to Dr. Wadsworth, to be addressed and forwarded to Philadelphia. It is quite consistent with her aversion to publicity in any form that she preferred not to subject her private correspondence to the scrutiny of a village postmaster. Although this is the first allusion in these letters to such an enclosure, the little service that Mrs. Holland performed may have begun some years before, when Dr. Wadsworth first returned from San Francisco to Philadelphia.

XXXVI

[1876]

I once more come, with my little Load – Is it too heavy, Sister?

You remember from whom I quoted, when you brought me the Clover?

"I find your Benefits no Burden, Jane."

Had I only a Postal, with your Smile, I should sleep safer.

Emily.

In similar writing now comes a poem which, after the paper was folded for enclosure, was addressed to Dr. Holland. It may have been sent in addition to the "little Load" in the above note, or enclosed with the letter that follows.

> No Passenger was known to flee –
> That lodged a Night in Memory.
> That wily – subterranean Inn
> Contrives that none go out again.
>
> Emily.

The Amherst weather records show that the summer of 1876 was unusually hot and dry. During July no rain fell, and the drought was only slightly relieved in August by a single thunderstorm of such violence that according to Emily's account of it to the Norcross sisters, the Dickinsons' clock stopped, "which," she said, "made it like Judgment Day" (*Letters*, p. 256).

A similar atmosphere seems to have prevailed when Emily and Lavinia received a call from their Aunt Elizabeth, Mrs. Augustus Currier of Worcester, who was their father's youngest sister. This lady does not appear to have been a favorite in the family, and Emily's characterization of her, placed in quotation marks, may have been a family saying.

With Lavinia's discovery of a pod on the sweet-pea vines to tell us that summer was nearing its end, we may infer that it was late in August when Emily wrote this letter to Mrs. Holland, who was away with her family on their summer vacation. It was probably in the summer of 1876 that the Hollands first visited Alexandria Bay, in the Thousand Island region of the Saint Lawrence, where they later made their permanent summer home. The person whom Emily bade call on them, whose name was deleted when the letter was first published, was doubtless Mrs. Austin Dickinson, who often visited her relatives in Geneva, New York. Sending her thoughts in the same direction toward two who were dear to her, Emily, who took little account of miles, might easily have pictured them as staying in adjacent towns.

XXXVII

[August 1876]

Loved and Little Sister, – Vinnie brought in a sweet pea today, which had a pod on the "off" side. Startled by the omen, I hasten to you.

An unexpected impediment to my reply to your dear last, was a call from my Aunt Elizabeth – "the only male relative on the female side," and though many days since, its flavor of court-martial still sets my spirit tingling.

With what dismay I read of those columns of kindred in the Bible – the Jacobites and the Jebusites and the Hittites and the Jacqueminots!

I am sure you are better, for no rheumatism in its senses would stay after the thermometer struck ninety!

We are revelling in a gorgeous drought.

The grass is painted brown, and how nature would look in other than the standard colors, we can all infer. . . I bade ——— call on you, but Vinnie said you were "the other side the globe," yet Vinnie thinks Vermont is in Asia, so I don't intend to be disheartened by trifles.

Vinnie has a new pussy that catches a mouse an hour. We call her the "minute hand" . . . .

In the autumn of 1876, Austin Dickinson visited the Centennial Exposition at Philadelphia and was stricken afterwards with a severe case of malaria from which he was slow to recover. From a sequence of three letters written close together soon after the critical phase of his illness was past, it appears that when he was convalescent the Hollands invited him to come and stay with them in New York. Mrs. Holland may have been at Amherst while he was ill, for in the first letter Emily refers to her friend's regret at not having heard a certain sermon, though she does not say who the preacher was or where he preached.

Since Emily, in these years, never attended church, one wonders whether it might have been a sermon of Dr. Wadsworth's to which she referred, rather than a sermon by one of the Amherst preachers. None of Dr. Wadsworth's published sermons, however, is on the subject Emily suggests, though it is possible that he sometimes sent her copies of those that were never put into print. But a sermon that does carry out the theme was preached at the opening of the Amherst College year, the sixteenth of September 1876, by Professor W. S. Tyler, who had a considerable reputation as a forceful and original speaker. Although the college archives contain a number of printed sermons by Professor Tyler, this one is not among them, and it is questionable whether Emily would have had a copy of it to lend. The suggestion is offered only because of the appropriateness of the subject.

According to a note in a college periodical, the *Amherst Student,* published shortly after this date, Professor Tyler's theme was from the text "The Sabbath was made for Man, not Man for the Sabbath" (Mark 2: 27). Although Emily's words "Corn in the Ear" suggest a different text (Mark 4: 28), they are also appropriate to the one Professor Tyler used. The first part of the passage, containing a question to which his text is the answer, reads, "And it came to pass that he went through the cornfields on the Sabbath Day, and his disciples began, as they went, to pluck the ears of corn. And the Pharisees said unto him, Behold, why do they on the Sabbath Day that which is unlawful?"

If this September sermon was the one to which Emily refers, considerable time had passed since she had seen Mrs. Holland, for when she next writes winter has set in with all its severity, and she turns eagerly to the warmth of companionship she feels in writing to her friend.

XXXVIII

[Winter 1876–1877]

Dear Sister.

I have felt so sweet an impatience to write you, that I thought it perhaps inordinate, and to be disciplined, like other unruly wishfulness – but however you stem Nature, she at last succeeds.

Your Letters have the peculiar worth that attaches to all prowess, as each is an achievement for your delicate Eyes. I almost fear you urge them too far, though to lag is stale to a rapid Spirit.

I hope you may live till I am asleep in my personal Grave, not but Earth is Heaven, but I would not like to outlive the smile on your guileless Face. Doctor's "Child Wife" – indeed – if not Mr Copperfield's.

This is a stern Winter, and in my Pearl Jail, I think of Sun and Summer as visages unknown.

The Sermon you failed to hear, I can lend you – though Legerdemain is unconveyed – and "Corn in the Ear," Audacity, these inclement Days.

I was much impressed by your sweetness to Austin. He seems the "Child of the Regiment" since he was so sick, and every tenderness to him is caress to us.

Congratulate the Doctor on his growing Fame.

"Stratford on Avon" – accept us all!

With love, for your sweet Descendants – and the wish for yourself, I am

Emily.

Emily was touched by the thoughtfulness of the Hollands' invitation to Austin, which may have been a casual one that did not call for an immediate answer. We may suppose that although she left it to Austin and his wife to make a conventional response, her next letter is an expression of the thought that had been evoked by her conversation with her brother about the proposed visit.

XXXIX

[Winter 1876–1877]

Saturday Night.

Austin will come tomorrow.

"Tomorrow," whose location
  The Wise deceives
Though it's hallucination
  Is last that leaves —
Tomorrow, thou Retriever
  Of every tare,
Of Alibi art thou
  Or ownest where?

Emily.

Mrs. Holland could not have taken the little poem literally, for Emily headed it "Saturday Night," and it could not have reached her at the earliest before the day *after* "tomorrow." But it may have left her uncertain as to whether or not to prepare the guest room for Austin some other day in the near future. Having heard nothing directly from him or his wife, she seems to have written to Emily to inquire. Emily's reply gives an explanation of their failure to answer the invitation.

Austin Dickinson had succeeded his father as treasurer of Amherst College, and he had become, as well, a leader in many of the affairs of the town, devoting both time and money to projects for its improvement. Pressing responsibilities awaited him as soon as he recovered from his illness. Mrs. Dickinson, busy though she was with her well-run home and active children, had sought other outlets for her keen mind, among which was a social life that brought her a reputation in a circle far beyond the limits of Amherst as a brilliant and charming hostess. In presenting their excuses, Emily found it necessary to offer an apology of her own.

XL

[Winter 1876–1877]

Will my little Sister excuse me?

"Douglass, Douglass, tender and true," who never swindled me! I am ashamed and sorry. I meant hypothetic tomorrows – though are there any other?

I deserve to be punished. I am – in regret.

Austin said he should write you, and that Sue w'd too – but he is overcharged with care, and Sue with scintillation, and I fear they have not.

Austin was pleased and surprised, that you wished for him, and still hopes he may go, but not now – but "Beyond," as the Vane says. You remember Little Nell's Grandfather leaned on his Cane on the Knoll that contained her, with "She will come tomorrow." That was the kind of tomorrow I meant.

I hope I have not tired "Sweetest Eyes were ever seen," for whose beloved acts, both revealed and covert, I am each Day more fondly, their Possessor's Own –

Early in the spring exchange of courtesies was carried on between the Dickinsons and the Hollands by the men of the families. When business took Dr. Holland within reach of Amherst, he wrote that he would drop in to see Emily and Lavinia, and the latter, with characteristic bustle, was prepared to be hospitable long before the time of his expected call.

Although Austin did not accept the Hollands' invitation to stay with them, he did go to New York, taking with him his daughter Martha, then ten years old. Father and daughter called on the Hollands, finding other visitors at the house whose presence seems to have caused them all so much amusement that Emily heard about the occasion from Mrs. Holland as well as from her brother. No information as to who they were has come to light, and Emily's comment leaves one guessing as to whether "those young Men" were uncouth specimens – admirers of Dr. Holland from the scene of one of his public appearances – or whether they were lighthearted members of a little circle, friends of Annie and Kate, of whom Hart Lyman, later editor of the New York Tribune, was the leading wit.

Mrs. Holland had written with enthusiasm of her minister, the Reverend Llewellyn Bevan of the Brick Presbyterian Church. The Dickinsons were also devoted to theirs, the Reverend Jonathan Jenkins. After ten years in Amherst, he left the parish in the spring of 1877, and his going was deeply regretted. He was a man of ardent religious faith, but his liberal views made it possible for him to accept Emily's divergence, and according to his son, MacGregor Jenkins, to report to her anxious father that he found her quite "sound" (*Emily Dickinson, Friend and Neighbor,* p. 82). Although she no longer went to church, Emily shared with the rest of her family a warm affection for Mr. and Mrs. Jenkins and their children.

XLI

[Early spring 1877]

Sister.

The vitality of your syllables compensates for their infrequency. There is not so much Life as *talk* of Life, as a general thing. Had we the first intimation of the Definition of Life, the calmest of us would be Lunatics!

Austin described his call in his own way, which was of course inimitable.

I hope those young Men have the supports of the Gospel, though that is a dim Elixir in cases like their's.

Austin said he was much ashamed of Mattie, and she was much ashamed of him, she imparted to us. They are a weird couple.

I am glad if you love your Clergyman, though the error to love our's has cost us severely.

God seems much more friendly through a hearty Lens.

There is a Dove in the Street and I own beautiful Mud – so I know Summer is coming. I was always attached to Mud, because of what it typifies – also, perhaps, a Child's tie to primeval Pies.

Vinnie put on fresh Cheeks three times, for the Doctor – but I thought I should have time to change mine, after he came –

As it proved, I did.

I hope you are both safe and in sweet health, and that at some stage of my swift career, I shall again meet you.

Were but our own immortal Mortals, as with us as Nature, we should demand few Alms.

Emily.

In the spring of 1877, Emily heard that Mrs. Holland was planning to spend the hot months at Alexandria Bay. An early spell of heat persuaded her that the time had arrived, and she did not wait for the calendar to declare the beginning of summer, but addressed a letter to the resort on the Saint Lawrence while the lilacs were still in bloom at Amherst. Mrs. Holland may indeed have been there to receive it, ready to carry out a project which was fulfilled later in the summer. The Holland family had been so delighted with the Thousand Island region when they first visited Alexandria Bay that they decided to make it their permanent summer home. In 1877 Dr. Holland bought a tract of fifteen acres on the mainland, across the bay from the village, and started to build a house on a high rocky point from which there was an uninterrupted view of the wide American channel and many of the wooded islands that reach toward the Canadian shore. The Dickinsons may have read the news in the *Springfield Republican,* where a somewhat inaccurate note in the "Gleanings and Gossip" column appeared on the twenty-third of July, saying, "Dr. Holland has bought an island in the St. Lawrence, and named it Bonny Castle. He intends to build a Swiss cottage on it."

XLII

[Late May 1877]

Dear friend.

I hesitate where you are, but decide to indite my Letter to my Sister in "Alexandria Bay," as the Irishman does to his "Mother in Dublin."

You have been magnanimous – and I requite you with nothing – the Sum that Benefactors love.

The Days are very hot and the Weeds pant like the centre of Summer. They say the Corn likes it. I thought there were others besides the Corn. How deeply I was deluded! Vinnie rocks her Garden and moans that God wont help her –

I suppose he is too busy, getting "angry with the Wicked – every Day."

He loves too homogeneously for Vinnie's special Mind.

Would you believe that our sacred Neighbors, the Mr and Mrs Sweetser, were so enamored of "Nicholas Minturn," that they borrow our Number before it is cold? But Youth, like Indian Summer, comes twice a Year –

Vinnie says I must go – or the Mail will leave me.

The etiquette of the admonition is questionable – though of it's imperativeness there is no doubt.

I must just show you a Bee, that is eating a Lilac at the Window. There – there – he is gone! How glad his family will be to see him!

Bees are Black, with Gilt Surcingles –
Buccaneers of Buzz.
Ride abroad in ostentation
And subsist on Fuzz.

Fuzz ordained – not Fuzz contingent –
Marrows of the Hill.
Jugs – a Universe's fracture
Could not jar or spill.

Emily.

After the summer on the Saint Lawrence was over, Mrs. Holland made a visit at Amherst of which Emily's next letter gives the echoes. Each member of the family in her separate way had found refreshment in her company, but of them all it was probably Lavinia who was most in need at this time of her friendly counsel. The exact nature of Lavinia's "woe" has not been revealed, but the seriousness of its effect is shown in the letter that follows this. Emily, whose sensitive inner life was impinged upon by the varied emotions of those who surrounded her so closely, found a refuge in Mrs. Holland's sanity and cheerful warmth.

XLIII

[Early autumn 1877]

I miss my little Sanctuary and her redeeming ways. A Savior in a Nut, is sweeter to the grasp than ponderous Prospectives.

Come again, and go not – which when a faithful invitation, is the sweetest known!

Mother pines for you, and says you were "so social." Mother misses power to ramble to her Neighbors – and the stale inflation of the minor News.

I wish the Sky and she had been better friends, for that is "sociability" that is fine and deathless.

How precious Thought and Speech are! "A present so divine," was in a Hymn they used to sing when I went to Church.

Vinnie talks of you –

Your cheerful view of Woe remodeled her's, I think – and Maggie deems you a Mistress most to be desired.

You see each looks at you through her specific Vista.

There is not yet Frost, and Vinnie's Garden from the Door looks like a Pond, with Sunset on it.

Bathing in that heals her.

How simple is Bethesda!

Love to your World – or Worlds.

Cheerfulness could not be permanently sustained in a world where woe was real. In addition to her constant attendance on her mother, an extra burden fell on Emily that winter in the illness of Lavinia. It is strange that no other letters have come to light that mention this "singular illness," which seems to have been the result of an emotional disturbance in Lavinia's personal relations, referred to in this letter as "torture." The fact that all the Dickinsons were highly excitable takes nothing from the reality of Lavinia's suffering. Mrs. Holland shared with Emily the knowledge of its cause, which was probably of too private a nature to be recorded on paper.

Emily was troubled too, and her sense of the imminence of death was sharpened at this time by the loss of an old family friend and the serious illness of another. Mrs. Lord, the wife of her father's closest friend, Judge Otis P. Lord of Salem, died on the tenth of December, 1877. The Lords had made frequent visits at the Dickinsons' house, and Emily had known them, since her childhood, almost as members of the family circle. But the death of one of the older generation could not be quite so poignantly felt as the threatened loss of a dear friend of her own age. Samuel Bowles, who had been a frequent and cherished guest in both the Dickinson houses, was gravely ill – worn out by the driving force of his own nature, which constantly pushed him beyond the slender limits of his nervous energy.

Under such a cloud of anxieties, it was natural that Emily should turn to the person who above all others had helped her in her spiritual struggles, so it is not surprising to find that she encloses a note for Dr. Wadsworth when she writes to Mrs. Holland early in January with the specific request that the note be forwarded to Philadelphia.

XLIV

[Early January 1878]

I always feel that the Minutest Effort of the dear Eyes, demands a peculiarly immediate reply – and internally it receives it, but time to say we are sorry, is sometimes withheld –

Wrenched from my usual Route by Vinnie's singular illness – and Mother's additional despair – I have felt like a troubled Top, that spun without reprieve. Vinnie's relief is slow. She has borne more than she could, as you and I know more of, than her Physician does.

Torture for worthless sakes is equally Torture.

I shall try superhumanly to save her, and believe I shall, but she has been too lacerated to revive immediately.

Mrs Lord – so often with us – has fled – as you know – Dear Mr Bowles is hesitating – God help him decide on the Mortal Side!

This is Night – now – but we are not dreaming. Hold fast to your Home, for the Darling's stealthy momentum makes each moment – Fear.

I enclose a Note, which if you would lift as far as Philadelphia, if it did not tire your Arms – would please me so much.

Would the Doctor be willing to address it? Ask him, with my love.

Maggie remembers you with fondness – and Mother gives her love — Vinnie longs for you.

Is not the distinction, of Affection, almost Realm enough?

Emily.

The spark of vitality in Samuel Bowles had burned too low to be revived, and he died on the sixteenth of January 1878, at the age of fifty-two. Though he was primarily her brother Austin's friend, Emily, who had captured his friendship for herself as well, found the loss of his vital personality hard to accept. Loving life with all its diversity, he poured himself out warmly and generously for his many friends. Unconventional in thought and startlingly honest, he sometimes made enemies in public life, but he attained eminence through his newspaper which held a unique place during the thirty years of his editorship. His biographer, George S. Merriam, said, "The great achievement of Samuel Bowles was that he built up under the limitations of a country town, a paying newspaper which expressed the editor's personal opinions, bound by no party, by no school, by no clique" (*Life and Times of Samuel Bowles,* p. 69).

Dr. Holland, too, must have felt the loss of his friend deeply. Speaking at the memorial service in Springfield, he told with the greatest simplicity of his relation with Mr. Bowles, which during the years when they worked together had been one of mutual respect rather than personal friendship. "After we separated our business interests," he said, "we came nearer together socially, and something warmer and tenderer took the place of the old respect. We had probably both mellowed a little through the influence of twenty-five years of experience and discipline. Indeed this discipline had given us something in common, and on its basis, stimulated by a remembrance of the old associations, we became hearty friends."

It is probable that Mr. Bowles would have been ready earlier for a warmer relation, and it may have been Dr. Holland's fear of his impetuosity that held it back. An inscription which Samuel Bowles wrote on the flyleaf of a copy of his book *Across the Continent,* which he gave to Dr. Holland in 1866, could hardly have expressed more appreciation: "To J. G. Holland, my pleasant and faithful associate through the most active and earnest years of my life; with whom I did my best work; for whose aims and ambitions I hold the largest respect, and for whose life and happiness I pray my best prayers and feel my tenderest love."

At the time of Mr. Bowles' death, Dr. Holland was not well, and when he was asked to speak at the service in Springfield he felt at first that it would be impossible for him to go. Then, remembering an instance of Mr. Bowles' friendship ten years before, when he had traveled from Chicago at great inconvenience to see the Holland family off for Europe, Dr. Holland decided to ignore his personal discomfort and take the risk of becoming ill from the effort, for the sake of honoring his friend. Soon after this a letter from Mrs. Holland brought Emily the disquieting news that Dr. Holland was in poor health. Although this was the first intimation of the heart trouble that took his life a few years later, at the beginning his condition does not appear to have been considered alarming. When she wrote, Mrs. Holland slipped into the letter a new photograph of herself in the small popular size of the period. Emily writes now to acknowledge it.

Although this is the first time she has spoken in these letters of

"Austin's Baby," the little boy whose late arrival gave him a special welcome in the family was already two and a half years old. By the time he was able to run back and forth between the two houses, he had completely won his Aunt Emily's heart. Her great attraction for children brought the two into a relation that gave her a special delight which no adult friendship could afford.

XLV

[Early 1878]

Your sweet Face alighted in the Rain, with it's Smile unharmed. All was there but Breath, and even that seemed optional – it was so confiding. Thank you for coming Home —

"Home – sweet Home" – Austin's Baby sings – "there is no place like Home – 'tis too – over to Aunt Vinnie's."

Thank you for Dr Gray's Opinion – that is peace – to us. I am sorry your Doctor is not well. I fear he has "improved" too many "shining Hours."

Give my love to him, and tell him the "Bee" is a reckless Guide. Dear Mr. Bowles found out too late, that Vitality costs itself.

How mournful without him! I often heard the Students sing – delicious Summer nights, "I've seen around me fall – like Leaves in wintry weather" — This was what they meant —

You kindly ask for Mother's health.

It is tranquil, though trifling. She reads a little – sleeps much – chats – perhaps – most of all – about nothing momentous, but things vital to her – and reminds one of Hawthorne's blameless Ship – that forgot the Port —

Vinnie is better – though sober – Maggie – invulnerable,

and loyal to you – Ned has brought his Hens to live in our Hen House, which adds to our little Group.

Three is a scant Assembly, but Love makes "One to carry –" as the Children say –

That is all of my Learning that I recall.

Tenderly,

Emily.

Mrs. Holland's next letter must have contained reassuring news in regard to her husband's health, for Emily wrote to congratulate him on his improvement. From her girlhood the theme of death seems always to have been present in the background of her thoughts, and her early letters were filled with pictures of a safe and pleasant heaven. It is natural that in maturity the emphasis should change, and after the death of her father, followed by that of Samuel Bowles, the insecurity of life and the question of what follows became more urgent and the picture more obscure. Sometimes, as in the following letter, it is hard to discover where she draws the line between "mortal" and "immortal."

XLVI

[Early 1878]

Dear Doctor,

We rejoice in your repaired health, though it grieves us that repairs should be necessary in a Structure so able – yet when we recall that the "Soul's poor Cottage battered and dismayed,* lets in new light through Chinks that time has made," your predicament becomes one of congratulation.

You seem to have reared Fames as rapidly as Houses, and

*[in margin] *decayed.*

we trust of more lasting ingredient, though the Abode without a Nail has it's consternations.

We hope that you are happy so far as Peace is possible to Mortal and immortal Life, for those ways "Madness lies."

"About" *which* "Ranks the Sunbeams play," is a touching question.

But I intrude on Sunset, and Father and Mr Bowles.

These held their Wick above the West,
Till when the Red declined –
Or how the Amber aided it –
Defied to be defined –

Then waned without disparagement
In a dissembling Hue
That would not let the Eye decide
Did it abide or no –

Emily.

From the first and last lines of the next letter we gather that Emily was enclosing another note to be forwarded to her friend in Philadelphia.

There was little of personal interest in the papers that escaped Emily's eye, and she usually discovered Dr. Holland's name when it appeared in print. In those days the literary columns of the daily papers carried critical comments on the current magazines just before they were issued. It may have been in such an item that Emily found the announcement she refers to of a picture of the Hollands' new house that was soon to appear. Though the reference has not been identified, there was a picture of the newly completed house in *Scribner's Monthly* for April, used as one of the illustrations drawn by Howard Pyle for an article he wrote about the Thousand Islands. No title is given to the picture, and the ownership of the house is not mentioned. One would prefer to identify the "portrait" Emily looked forward to seeing with an article that appeared in the *Springfield Republican* on the twenty-fourth of the following July, with the heading, "From the Thousand Islands. A Picture of Dr. Holland's Bonnie Castle," by Clark Bryan, a former business partner of Dr. Holland's in the *Republican's* firm. The article describes a visit to the summer resort, where the writer stayed with the Hollands, and contains a detailed description of the new house. At that time, however, it would be difficult to account for an allusion in Emily's letter to a recent visit from Mrs. Holland, who seems to have surprised the sisters by a brief call. Lavinia's comparison of her to Talleyrand suggests that she had been staying with her cousins in Northampton and had found it necessary to use strategy to absent herself from them long enough to drive over to Amherst. In view of the visit, it has seemed best tentatively to choose March as the date for the letter.

XLVII

[March? 1878]

Dear Sister.

I take Mrs. Browning's little Basket to bring the note to you – and when you find it is not her, you will be disappointed, but there is many a discipline before we obtain Heaven. Your little Note protected, as it always does, and the "Whips of Time" felt a long way off.

Your little Trip still lingers, for is not all petite you do – you are such a Linnet?

Vinnie was much elated by your rogueries. She thinks you are stealthy as Talleyrand –

We learn of you in the Papers and of your new House, of which it is said there will be a Portrait – "so I shall see it in just three Days," though I would rather see it's vital inhabitants.

I gave your words to Ned – who bowed and seemed much raised –

Baby does all the errands now – and I enclose a Circular, setting forth his wants.

To see the little Missionary starting with his Basket, would warm the chillest Heart.

I know you will do what I ask you, and so I only thank you, and make no outer remarks.

Lovingly,

Emily.

When spring came, its beauty seemed to make more poignant to Emily the grief she felt in the loss of the family friend, Samuel Bowles, who in other springs had come to Austin Dickinson's house at blossom time. In earlier springs Mrs. Holland had sent bunches of trailing arbutus, the spring's earliest flowers, picked under her own pines at Brightwood. Emily as a girl had searched them out for herself in her favorite haunts in the woods. To send her a bunch of the "Pink, small and punctual" flowers from New York, where perhaps Mrs. Holland bought them from a street vendor, was a playful gesture which she must have known Emily would enjoy.

XLVIII

[Spring 1878]

I thought that "Birnam Wood" had "come to Dunsinane." Where did you pick arbutus? In Broadway, I suppose. They say that God is everywhere, and yet we always think of Him as somewhat of a recluse. . . It is hard not to hear again that vital "Sam is coming" – though if grief is a test of a priceless life, he is compensated. He was not ambitious for redemption – that was why it is his. "To him that hath, shall be given." Were it not for the eyes, we would know of you oftener. Have they no remorse for their selfishness? "This tabernacle" is a blissful trial, but the bliss predominates.

I suppose you will play in the water at Alexandria Bay, as the baby does at the tub in the drive. . . Speak to us when your eyes can spare you, and "keep us, at home, or by the way," as the clergyman says, when he folds the church till another Sabbath.

Before Mrs. Holland left New York in June with the prospect of a happy summer at Bonniecastle before her, she sent a box of chocolates to Emily and Lavinia, who were tied to the changeless routine of caring for their invalid mother.

Perhaps Dr. Holland's acceptance of the physical limitations imposed on him by his heart ailment intensified his enjoyment of the good things life had brought him, for the summers at Bonniecastle were remembered by his family as a time of fulfillment for him. The house was always full of guests, young and old. He bought a small steam launch which was later superseded by a larger yacht, built to order. The contract, still in the editor's possession, guarantees a speed of fifteen knots an hour. To the alarm of his family, who were fearful of the strain on his heart, he sometimes indulged in races, to prove his yacht the fastest on the river. He delighted in the rocks and the water, the pines, spruces, and birches, a lawn where the young people played tennis and croquet, and a well-tended vegetable garden. He also took an interest in the affairs of the village in which the public library still bears his name.

In writing her thanks for the gift, Emily noted, with characteristic emphasis on the mystery of death, the passing on the twelfth of June of William Cullen Bryant, whom Dr. Holland counted as one of his closest literary friends.

XLIX

[June 1878]

I thought it was you, little Chocolate Sister – but Vinnie demurred – and Vinnie decides. I said "let me thank her conditionally" – "No" – said Vinnie –" 'twould be remorse – provided it were not her – " and so we guessed and sighed and nibbled and propounded – and felt how base we were – until the Doctor's note.

The Bonbons were delightful, but better than Bonbons was the love – for that is the basis of Bonbons. And in all the confusion to think of us – Loyal little Sister – the Bird going South is not so mindful of the Birds behind. To never forget you – is all we can –

That is how faint a Stipend –

The Doctor's Pun was happy – How lovely are the wiles of Words!

We thought you cherished Bryant, and spoke of you immediately when we heard his fate – if Immortality *be* Fate.

Dear friends – we cannot believe for each other. I suppose there are depths in every Consciousness, from which we cannot rescue ourselves – to which none can go with us – which represent to us Mortally – the Adventure of Death.

How unspeakably sweet and solemn – that whatever await us of Doom or Home, we are mentally permanent.

"It is finished" can never be said of us.

I am glad of your bright Home –

I hope you are well – you did not tell me – Thank you peculiarly sweetly – With grief for the eyes only, happy for your happiness,

Emily.

It was not long after Emily had written the foregoing letter that her mother suffered the accident that made her a permanent invalid. More closely confined than before, Emily seems to have been too preoccupied to write to Mrs. Holland for several months, though she alludes in the next letter to one she had recently written – perhaps as a Christmas greeting – which is missing from the collection. Mrs. Holland's usual Christmas gift, a box of chocolates, may have been delayed in coming, for Emily wrote about the middle of January to tell of its arrival. She seems to have gone straight from her daily reading of the newspaper to her desk, for there are two allusions to items of importance mentioned in the current papers, the facts of which are given in the notes to this letter.

L

[Mid-January 1879]

The lovely little Bronzes in the Lace House – came just as I had written you.

The deference to my predilection pleased and smote me too.

I am glad you are not hung – like the "Mollie Maguires," tho' doubtless heinous as themselves – in a sweet way.

Austin's Baby says when surprised by statements – "There's – *sum*th*h*n–else – there's – *Bum*b*ul* – Beese."

God's little Blond Blessing – we have long deemed you, and hope his so called "Will" – will not compel him to revoke you.

The "rectification of his Frontier," costs the Earth too much.

Vinnie and I watch Mother, which makes the Days too short – till we wear the same Heart – Day and Night, and wash our Hand with our Tongue as the Pussy does. I shall not write again for a few moments, which will defray your cares. Vinnie wants to write, but was it "Atlas'" fault the World was on his Shoulders?

Mother and Sister give their love, and let my own preponderate –

Emily.

When Emily wrote the next autumn in response to a long overdue letter from Mrs. Holland – which had broken an almost embarrassing silence – she was gently reproachful. No events of importance had occurred in either family during the interval. Dr. Holland's uncertain health had made it seem wise for him to turn over some of the responsibility he had carried for the magazine to his able associates, but he still lived a full and active life. Mrs. Dickinson, on the other hand, had failed to improve, and the sameness of Emily's days must have made the gap in communications seem even longer than it had been in reality.

LI

[October 1879]

Little Sister,

I was glad you wrote. I was just about addressing the Coroner of Alexandria – You spared me the melancholy research.

Are you pretty well – have you been happy –

Are your Eyes safe?

A thousand questions rise to my lips, and as suddenly ebb – for how little I know of you recently – An awkward loneliness smites me – I fear I must ask with Mr Wentworth, "Where are our moral foundations?"

Should you ask what had happened here, I should say nothing perceptible. Sweet latent events – too shy to confide –

It will vivify us to your remembrance to tell you that Austin and Sue have just returned from Belchertown Cattle Show.

Austin brought me a Balloon and Vinnie a Watermelon and each of his family a Whip. Wasn't it primitive?

When they drove away in the dust this morning, I told them they looked like Mr and Mrs "Pendexter," turning their backs upon Longfellow's Parish.

Brave Vinnie is well. Mother does not yet stand alone and fears she never shall walk, but I tell her we all shall fly so soon, not to let it grieve her, and what indeed is Earth but a Nest, from whose rim we are all falling?

One day last Summer I laughed once like "Little Mrs Holland," Vinnie said I did – how much it pleased us all.

I ask you to ask your Doctor will he be so kind as to write the name of my Philadelphia friend on the Note within, and your little Hand will take it to him.

You were so long so faithful, Earth would not seem homelike without your little sunny Acts.

Love for you each –

Emily.

Emily now spent much of her time in attendance on her mother, and her writing was done late at night. Although the following letter was written nine months later than the preceding one, the intimations are that there had been others in the interval. One little note, in which Emily asked a question that was of importance to her, seems never to have reached its destination, and though she was disappointed not to receive an answer to it, she did not ask the question again.

Many of the hours spent at her mother's bedside must have been tedious, but as this letter shows, the conversations she carried on there were not always restricted to the invalid's range. Emily often turned to her brother Austin for companionship in her thoughts, finding him congenially unorthodox. He remained an active church member, but was sufficiently heretical to be accused by some of the local conservatives of atheistic tendencies, though his close friend Mr. Jenkins had declared that he was simply fifty years ahead of his time (*Emily Dickinson Face to Face*, p. 133).

LII

[4 July 1880]

July 4th

Dear friend,

While Little Boys are commemorating the advent of their Country, I have a Letter from "Aunt Glegg" saying "Summer is nearly gone," so I thought I would pick a few Seeds this Afternoon and bid you Good bye as you would be off for Winter. I think Persons dont talk about "Summer stopping" this time o' year, unless they are inclement themselves.

I wish you would speak to the Thermometer about it – I dont like to take the responsibility.

Perhaps you never received a Note I sent you or you would have answered the little question was in it?

It was not about the "promised Messiah."

The Weather is like Africa and the Flowers like Asia and the Numidian Heart of your "Little Friend" neither slow nor chill.

The Road to Paradise is plain,
And holds scarce* one.
Not that it is not firm
But we presume
A Dimpled Road

* originally *just,* then erased.

Is more preferred.
The Belles of Paradise are few –
Not me – nor you –
But unsuspected things –
Mines have no Wings.

July 15th

You see I have been delayed — but we will begin where we left off.

Austin and I were talking the other Night about the Extension of Consciousness, after Death and Mother told Vinnie, afterward, she thought it was "very improper."

She forgets that we are past "Correction in Righteousness."

I dont know what she would think if she knew that Austin told me confidentially "there was no such person as Elijah."

I suppose Doctor is catching Trout and Convalescence and wish I could meet them both at Breakfast – and bid my very little Sister a most sweet Good Night.

Later in the summer Mrs. Holland answered, inviting Emily to repeat the question that had been lost. From an allusion in Emily's next letter we may gather that Mrs. Holland described the flower beds she had laid out among the rocks at Bonniecastle, where the soil was too shallow for perennials, but where poppies, nasturtiums, and other annuals made gay spots of color. It was after the first September frosts and while the hot political campaigns of a presidential election year were reaching their height that Emily wrote again. It is regrettable that by this time she found herself unable to repeat the question.

LIII

[September 1880]

Dear Sister.

The responsibility of Pathos is almost more than the responsibility of Care. Mother will never walk. She still makes her little Voyages from her Bed to her Chair in a Strong Man's Arms – probably that will be all.

Her poor Patience loses it's way and we lead it back. I was telling her Nieces yesterday, who wrote to ask for her, that to read to her – to fan her – to tell her "Health would come Tomorrow," and make the Counterfeit look real – to explain *why* "the Grasshopper is a Burden" — because it is not as new a Grasshopper as it was – this is so ensuing, that I hardly have said, "Good Morning, Mother," when I hear myself saying "Mother, – Good Night."

Time is short and full, like an outgrown Frock.

You are very kind to give me leave to ask "the question" again, but on renewed self-examination I find I have not the temerity.

I thought of your Garden in the Rocks those unfeeling Nights – perhaps it had "Watchers" as Vinnie's did.

I hope the Doctor is improving – in his health – I mean – his other perfections precluding the suggestion, and that my little Sister is in sweet robustness.

Vinnie is far more hurried than Presidential Candidates – I trust in more distinguished ways, for *they* have only the care of the Union, but Vinnie the Universe —

With her love and mine,

Emily.

In spite of the peaceful summers at Bonniecastle, the condition of Dr. Holland's health remained precarious, and about Thanksgiving time Mrs. Holland wrote that he had been ill again. Ever sympathetic, Emily soon replied, but the wording of her letter suggests that the acute phase of his attack had passed before she heard of it.

At the time she wrote all Amherst had been shocked by the untimely death of a brilliant young man, Elihu Root, who at the age of thirty-five was professor of mathematics and philosophy at Amherst College. Bearing the same name as the eminent lawyer and statesman to whom he was distantly related, he was the son of a cousin of Dr. Holland's. A memorial address presents him as eager and patient in his pursuit of truth, and a man whom everyone remembered for his guileless character, sympathetic nature, and just mind. His death occurred on the third of December, which fell on a Friday, and Emily's letter was written between that date and the day of his burial, which she said was to take place the following Tuesday. Assuming that she wrote on Sunday, as she often did, we can be almost certain of an exact date for this letter.

LIV

[5? December 1880]

Yes, Little Sister – we "thought of you" and had not quite finished, but shall resume at intervals, while you live, and we.

I trust the "Hand" has "ceased from troubling" – it has saved too many to be assailed by an "envious sliver."

Had we known the Doctor was falling, we had been much alarmed, though Grace – perhaps – is the only hight from which falling is fatal.

Each of us wish the Doctor were stronger – three importunities, tell him, to recover immediately.

The Snow is so white and sudden it seems almost like a Change of Heart – though I don't mean a "Conversion" – I mean a Revolution.

We had a timid Thanksgiving together. Mother didn't cry much, which pleased us very much – but the Sweet of the Day was in sending a Crumb to a poor fluttering Life, a few Boughs from our own, which will soon pass from our privilege.

The dying of your Kinsman Root, has bereaved the Village. He was exceedingly cherished by both Townsmen and Scholars – and thirteen Cars of Comrades take him Home next Tuesday.

The career of a Taper, I infer, though I never met him.

Austin is much won by his dying – he only knew him technically, till Election Day – when a few moments of sudden honor disclosed his farther Nature. There was great effort to save him, but the "Life saving Service" was impotent.

I trust we are grateful for the Life that sees – and steps – and touches, if it is only the thrilling preface to supremer things. Very lovely in Little Sister to transfer the particulars. Am not unmindful of the Dew or it's fervent circuit.

Fondly,

Emily.

When Emily wrote to thank the Hollands for a Christmas gift, which arrived late, with no indication of the names of the donors, death was again uppermost in her mind. Two more persons were gone who had meant much to her in different ways.

George Eliot, whose characters were as real to her as living persons, and for whom she felt an attachment almost as strong as that to Mrs. Browning, died the twenty-second of December 1880. A few days later Dr. David P. Smith, almost certainly the man to whom Emily alluded as "our Family Savior," died in Springfield.

Dr. Smith was one of a notable family of physicians. In addition to his wide practice he was a lecturer at the Yale Medical School, but he always kept his home in Springfield, where he was a friend of Samuel Bowles and a member of "The Club" to which both Mr. Bowles and Dr. Holland belonged. He must have been often at Amherst, for he was constantly called to widely separated places and sometimes traveled as much as two hundred miles in a day. He probably visited the Dickinsons only as a consultant, for two years after his death, Emily wrote of the doctor who attended her mother in her last illness as one with whom she had had long associations. Dr. Smith was greatly esteemed as a citizen of Springfield and his death was a loss to the whole Connecticut Valley region. He died on Sunday, December twenty-sixth, and Emily's letter was written the following Tuesday.

LV

[28 December 1880]

Tuesday –

Was it the Brother –

Was it the Sister –

Was it the Two One – that conflicting Numeral? Not in this instance conflicting. Oh No. Cupid forbid!

The Honey reached us yesterday.

Honey not born of Bee – but Constancy – which is "far better." I can scarcely tell you the sweetness it woke, nor the sweetness it stilled.

Grieving for "George Eliot" – grieved for Dr Smith, our Family Savior, living Fingers that are left, have a strange warmth.

It is deep to live to experience "And there was no more Sea" – the Fathom though is a daily one and traversed by the simplest Child. I hope you are both hopeful.

My Two give you their love, and my part of one, her docile respects.

I trust Doctor is stronger.

"As thy Day so shall thy Strength be" is an elastic ratio.

Please "consider" me – An antique request, though in behalf of Lilies.

Lovingly,

Emily.

Mrs. Holland must have answered Emily's inquiry about the "Honey" almost at once, and in giving news of the family she had told of the diamond earrings she had received as a Christmas gift from her hsuband. It had doubtless been a gay holiday season in New York, and Dr. Holland had been well enough to enjoy it. The custom of keeping "open house" on New Year's Day was still popular, and Mrs. Holland and the girls spent the day receiving calls from their friends young and old.

At Amherst there was scarcely a break in the routine of the three women in their quiet home, but Emily was acutely aware of the changes continually wrought in nature by the passage of the seasons. The year had closed dramatically with a partial eclipse of the sun on the thirty-first of December, and the new year opened with several days of intense cold, which clothed the dead flower stalks in Emily's garden with frost crystals.

LVI

[Early January 1881]

Sister Golconda must look very burnished in her Christmas Gifts, and the bashful Gem that the Scripture enjoins, "a meek and lowly Spirit," must be quite obscured – but one must clad demurely to please the Scripture's taste, a very plain Old Gentleman, with few Expenses out.

Your sweet light-hearted manner informed me more than statements, that the Doctor was better – the inferential Knowledge – the distinctest one, and I congratulate you – and not omit ourselves.

How sweet the "Life that now is," and how rugged to leave it – and ruggeder to stay behind when our Dear go.

A Little Boy ran away from Amherst a few Days ago, and when asked where he was going, replied, "Vermont or Asia." Many of us go farther. My pathetic Crusoe –

Vinnie had four Pussies for Christmas Gifts – and two from her Maker, previous, making six, in toto, and finding Assassins for them, is my stealthy Aim. Mother, we think unchanged – Vinnie's ideal "Irons" in the ideal "Fire" and me, prancing between – a Gymnastic Destiny.

Vails of Kamtchatka dim the Rose – in my Puritan Garden, and as a farther stimulus, I had an Eclipse of the Sun a few Mornings ago, but every Crape is charmed.

I knew a Bird that would sing as firm in the centre of Dissolution, as in it's Father's nest.

Phenix, or the Robin?

While I leave you to guess, I will take Mother her Tea.

Emily.

Sometimes Lavinia as well as Emily was moved to write to Mrs. Holland, but she lived so entirely in the world of tangible things that she was less able to turn from them and find spare moments in which to carry out her intention. Without a word of complaint about her sister, Emily explained in the next letter why she had failed to send one she had written earlier, when Vinnie begged her to wait until she had time to enclose a note of her own. Emily's deep attachment to the younger sister on whom in matters of daily living she was so dependent is nowhere more clearly or warmly expressed than here. When she writes again she encloses a note to be forwarded to Dr. Wadsworth.

LVII

[Early 1881]

A Letter was lying warm in my Pocket for my Little Sister, when her Letter came, but had delayed a Night for Vinnie, as is the melancholy case in many instances. I feel so punctual hearted I think I cannot wait, but an appeal from Vinnie, and I will sit in Love's Back Seat, and let the Horses walk.

I am glad that the dear Doctor has the Angel Wife, and not the Bride of Socrates to frown at tired Strength and make the weakness lonely – and *Prudence* is a tedious one, and needs beguiling – too. "Give me Liberty or give me Death" has a willful meaning – but never mind the "Liberty" for a few wise Days, then Doctor can "go Barefoot," and rollick with the best of us.

You always seemed to me like David and Goliath, and if Goliath is not as strong, David is needed more, but David is competent – in his – her – small – pathetic Hands, there is strength for both. The latent Sinew of the Love is faithful when 'tis called, and let it lurk till then.

I ask Mother "what message" she sends. She says, "Tell them I wish I could take them both in my Arms and carry them."

I never before have heard her speak so – those were the very words.

Will you let me take hold of your Hand to lead this little Note to the Mail?

Keeping you and the Doctor in beloved thought – you know who I am.

In spite of Dr. Holland's periods of ill health he never relaxed his active interest in the magazine he had built up. Late in 1880, however, he felt that it was time to free himself from some of his responsibility, and decided to sell his financial interests to his partner and members of his staff, while continuing as editor of the magazine. A reorganization followed in which the company, always distinct from the house of Scribner, changed its name to the Century Company. The magazine continued under the name *The Century*, but Dr. Holland lived to edit only the first issue, November 1881, which came out shortly after his death.

In spite of the relief from business responsibility, however, he was obliged to take frequent periods of rest. Emily's implication, in the last letter, that he was rebellious against the necessary restrictions on his activity, brought a sprightly reply from the Doctor himself, clearing him of the charge. His note was enough of an event to be shared with the family next door, and when they read it together it evoked a nostalgic atmosphere. Later years had brought to Susan Dickinson many new friends who were unknown to Emily, but Dr. Holland's letter brought back memories which the sisters-in-law shared and cherished equally.

LVIII

[Early 1881]

Dear Doctor,

Your small Note was as merry as Honey, and enthralled us all. I sent it over to Sue, who took Ned's Arm and came across – and we talked of Mr Samuel and you, and vital times when you two bore the Republican, and came as near sighing – all of us – as would be often wise – I should say next door. Sue said she was homesick for those "better Days," hallowed be their name.

Amazing Human Heart – a syllable can make to quake like jostled Tree – what Infinite – for thee!

I wish you were rugged, and rejoice you are gay, and am re-convinced by your arch note that Unless we become as Rogues, we cannot enter the Kingdom of Heaven.

Emily.

In the desolate interval between the official beginning of spring and the actual arrival of the birds Emily gives a picture of the household and its environment as it is affected by the season. Lavinia has taken refuge in a seed catalogue, while the neighborhood amuses itself with a serial story by Frances Hodgson Burnett which was running in the February, March, and April numbers of *Scribner's Monthly*.

LIX

[Late March 1881]

Dear Sister,

Spring, and not a Blue Bird, but I have seen a Crow – "in his own Body on the Tree," almost as prima facie.

They love such outlawed Trees.

An Antiquated Tree
Is cherished of the Crow
Because that Junior Foliage is disrespectful now
To venerable Birds
Whose Corporation Coat
Would decorate Oblivion's
Remotest Consulate.

Could you condone the profanity?

We have had two Hurricanes since the "Ides of March," and one of them came near enough to untie My Apron – a boldness please resent.

Mother is lying changeless on her changeless Bed, hoping a little, and fearing much – Vinnie in Bliss' Catalogue, prospecting for Summer.

You and I can content ourselves with only "Bliss" itself. What a parsimony! Maggie, good and noisy, the North Wind of the Family, but Sweets without a Salt would at last cloy.

The Neighborhood are much amused by the "Fair Barbarian" and Emily's Scribner is perused by all the Boys and Girls.

Even the Cynic Austin confessed himself amused.

I hope the Little Sister's Eyes have refrained from sighing – and very often carry them to the "Throne" of Tenderness – the only God I know – and if I take her too, it doesn't break My Basket, though Fondness' untold Load does tire rugged Baskets some.

I hope that nothing makes you afraid. Give my Heart to each, and my slim Circumference to her who often shared it.

Lovingly,

Emily.

Later in the spring Emily gaily used Lavinia's involvement in a household dilemma as an excuse for a letter in which the principal item of news was the death of a man who had long worked for her father. One might infer from the fact that she set his name "Horace" in quotation marks that the Dickinsons had called him, for reasons of their own, after the poet of the Sabine Hills. But it is quite safe to identify this village character with the "Horace Church, gardner" whose death on the seventh of April 1881 was entered in the Amherst town records. Emily's statement that this man had lived with them always does not mean that he was a household servant, for his name appears in the Amherst Directory for 1879 as farmer and sexton of the Congregational Church, which the Dickinsons attended. Perhaps it was the inconvenience of his last name in connection with his duties as sexton that caused him to be known throughout the town simply as "Horace." MacGregor Jenkins recalled the fascination he held for small boys because he wore a wig and a glass eye, and had at one time knocked out the village bully. For him, working for the Squire would not have been a matter of taking orders as it would have been for mere laborers like Dick or Pat. Though the independent villager of New England consents to earn his living by working for his well-to-do neighbors, he is quite likely to maintain his own opinions as to how the work should be carried out.

The legendary character which Emily imputes to Horace was not a matter of years, since he was only fifty-five at the time of his death. The dates she quotes from his reminiscences show him to have gained his position as a village character through his personal qualities, one of which was an imaginative memory.

LX

[Spring 1881]

Dear Sister.

We are making a few simple repairs, what Dickens would call qualifications and aspects – and looking in Vinnie's Basket for the Lightning Rod, which she had mislaid, "What *would* Mrs Holland think" said Vinnie?

"I would inquire," I said.

I can always rely on your little Laugh, which is what the Essayist calls "the immortal Peewee."

Did you know that Father's "Horace" had died – the "Cap'n Cuttle" of Amherst? He had lived with us always, though was not congenial – so his loss is a pang to Tradition, rather than Affection. I am sure you remember him. He is the one who spoke patronizingly of the Years, of Trees he sowed in "26," or Frosts he met in "20," and was so legendary that it seems like the death of the College Tower, our first Antiquity. I remember he was at one time disinclined to gather the Winter Vegetables till they had frozen, and when Father demurred, he replied "Squire, ef the Frost is the Lord's Will, I dont popose to stan in the way of it." I hope a nearer inspection of that "Will" has left him with as ardent a bias in it's favor.

Vinnie is under terrific headway, but finds time to remember you with vivid affection – and Mother is unchanged, though my new gratitude every morning, that she is still with us, convinces me of her frailty.

Vinnie is eager to see the Face of George Eliot which the Doctor promised, and I wince in prospective, lest it be no more sweet. God chooses repellant settings, dont he, for his best Gems?

All you will say of yourselves is dear to Emily and Vinnie, and is'nt to say it soon – prudent – in so short a Life?

The friends must have corresponded during the summer before Emily wrote the letter that follows here, for she alludes to the "duplicity" to which Mrs. Holland had consented. The only duplicity appearing in the letters is the innocent one of which she had written a year earlier (L), saying she had told her mother "health would come tomorrow." Perhaps Mrs. Holland had taken part in the effort to continue the deception, sending cheering messages to the helpless invalid.

Through more than two months that summer, the whole nation watched the papers anxiously for news of the condition of President

Garfield, who was shot on the second of July by a disappointed office seeker. Emily found companionship in the thought that when she was reading her paper, her friend was doing the same. She also read *Scribner's Monthly,* but was greatly disappointed in the latest story by William Dean Howells called *A Fearful Responsibility,* which appeared in the July and August numbers. In the August number she found a poem Dr. Holland had written to his dog, Blanco, a pure white English setter who was his constant companion in his last years.

LXI

[August 1881]

Dear Sister.

I think everything will get ripe Today so it can be Autumn tomorrow if it would like, for such heat was never present and I think of your Forest and Sea as a far off Sherbet.

We have an artificial Sea, and to see the Birds follow the Hose for a Crumb of Water is a touching Sight. They wont take it if I hand it to them – they run and shriek as if they were being assassinated, but oh, to steal it, that is bliss. I cant say that their views are not current.

When I look in the Morning Paper to see how the President is, I know you are looking too, and for once in the Day I am sure where you are, which is very friendly.

The Pilgrim's Empire seems to stoop – I hope it will not fall.

We have a new Black Man and are looking for a Philanthropist to direct him, because every time he presents himself, I run, and when the Head of the Nation shies, it confuses the Foot.

When you read in the "Massachusetts items" that he has eaten us up, a memorial merriment will invest these preliminaries.

Who wrote Mr Howells' story? Certainly he did not. Shakespeare was never accused of writing Bacon's works, though to have been suspected of writing his, was the most beautiful stigma of Bacon's Life. Higher, is the doom of the High.

Doctor's betrothal to "Blanco" I trust you bear unmurmuringly. Mother and Vinnie wept – I read it to both at their request.

Thank you for surviving the duplicity. Thank you for not stopping being anxious about us. Not to outgrow Suspense, is beloved indeed.

Emily.

Mrs. Holland seems to have been touched by Emily's account of the tears her mother and Lavinia had shed over Dr. Holland's poem about his dog and had sent them a photograph showing her husband and Blanco together. The letter that accompanied it contained the news that Annie had become engaged to John Howe of Troy, New York. An impending break in the family solidarity was, as Emily knew, of momentous importance, but she was not able to send her congratulations and sympathy at once because of the presence of friends who were staying at the hotel.

The register of the Amherst House was unfortunately destroyed in a later fire, and the effort to identify Emily's friends has proved unavailing. The local paper, the *Amherst Gazette,* lists the names of only a few of the hotel guests that summer, and no names appear on it that seem to have any connection with the Dickinsons. On the third of August the paper noted that the Reverend J. L. Jenkins and family were stopping in town as the guests of Austin Dickinson, but in view of the close intimacy between the two families, it would be strange if they were accommodated at the hotel. The word "duty" which Emily uses in regard to her relation to the visitors points rather to the visit she recounted to the Norcross sisters in a letter that seems to have been written a little later in the same season (*Letters*, p. 264). Family connections were involved, and clashes of personality were delightedly observed by Emily, whose sense of drama brought her secret pleasure. Among the group were her old friend Judge Lord and her aunt Lucretia Bullard, but since the other names have been deleted, it has been impossible to identify the lady and her daughter who seem to have been the cause of the friction.

LXII

[Late summer 1881]

Dear Sister,

What must you have thought that no one wrote? My Will did write immediately, but friends who were boarding at the Hotel claimed every moment that Duty could give till this Moment's Mail.

Thank you for apprizing us of the sweet Disaster in your family, which I trust you will meet as you meet all, with sunny heroism – and present our beatific congratulations to Annie. The impulse to write her myself, is strong as gravitation, but I know how busy the Heart is when it is very busy, and think it unkind to disturb her. Cupid still drives the Pink Coupe he did when we were Children, though I fear his affecting toils are not what Mrs Micawber would call "remunerative." I rejoice that Annie is happy.

To flee from the "Family Tree" is an innovation, but Birds are predatory. I am glad that you feel so sweetly toward the invading powers.

If the "Ark of the Lord" must be "taken," one has a choice in the Foe.

Your picture of Doctor was very ensnaring, but I remembered my rectitudes – though Vinnie, even at this distance, is captivated by the Dog.

Fascination is portable.

Today is parched and handsome, though the Grass is the color of Statesmen's Shoes, and only the Butterfly rises to the situation.

His little Body glistens with crispness – an ell of rapture to an inch of Wing.

I hope my little Sister is well, and her Best better, and be sure we are glad of the Happiness and each give it our love.

Emily.

Although both Dr. Holland and his wife knew that his heart ailment was incurable, there was no intimation that death was near until the final attack came. He returned to the city the fifth of October, feeling stronger than for some time past. On the eleventh he spent the day in his office, as usual, and on the way home called at John La-Farge's studio to see some new stained glass. Early in the morning of Wednesday, the twelfth, he was wakened by a sudden pain and lapsed into a brief unconsciousness from which he passed peacefully into death.

A telegram was sent to the Dickinsons, and Emily poured out her tender sympathy to Mrs. Holland in three letters, written in quick succession. The first letter may have been written that very day, the second only a day or two after, and the third on Thursday of the following week. In the third letter she inquired about the circumstances of Dr. Holland's death, and having received a reply she wrote once more. In order to preserve their continuity as parts of a whole – the spontaneous expression of the sorrow and solicitude that filled Emily's heart during those first days – these four letters have been printed as a group without further comment.

THE DICKINSON HOME · AMHERST · 1858

DR. HOLLAND

MRS. HOLLAND

LXIII

[13? October 1881]

We read the words but know them not. We are too frightened with sorrow. If that dear, tired one must sleep, could we not see him first?

Heaven is but a little way to one who gave it, here. "Inasmuch," to him, how tenderly fulfilled!

Our hearts have flown to you before — our breaking voices follow. How can we wait to take you all in our sheltering arms?

Could there be new tenderness, it would be for you, but the heart is full — another throb would split it — nor would we dare to speak to those whom such a grief removes, but we have somewhere heard "A little child shall lead them."

Emily.

LXIV

[15? October 1881]

Panting to help the dear ones and yet not knowing how, lest any voice bereave them but that loved voice that will not come, if I can rest them, here is down — or rescue, here is power.

One who only said "I am sorry" helped me the most when father ceased — it was too soon for language.

Fearing to tell mother, some one disclosed it unknown to us. Weeping bitterly, we tried to console her. She only replied "I loved him so."

Had he a tenderer eulogy?

Emily.

LXV

[20 October 1881]

Thursday.

After a while, dear, you will remember that there is a heaven — but you can't now. Jesus will excuse it. He will remember his shorn lamb.

The lost one was on such childlike terms with the Father in Heaven. He has passed from confiding to comprehending — perhaps but a step.

The *safety* of a beloved lost is the first anguish. With you, that is peace.

I shall never forget the Doctor's prayer, my first morning with you — so simple, so believing. *That* God must be a friend — *that* was a different God — and I almost felt warmer myself, in the midst of a tie so sunshiny.

I am yearning to know if he knew he was fleeing — if he spoke to you. Dare I ask if he suffered? Some one will tell me a very little, when they have the strength. . . Cling tight to the hearts that will not let you fall.

Emily.

LXVI

[Late October 1881]

. . . I know you will live for our sake, dear, you would not be willing to for your own. That is the duty which saves. While we are trying for others, power of life comes back, very faint at first, like the new bird, but by and by it has wings.

How sweetly you have comforted me — the toil to comfort you, I hoped never would come. A sorrow on your sunny face is too dark a miracle — but how sweet that he rose in the morning — accompanied by dawn. How lovely that he spoke with you, that memorial time! How gentle that he left the pang he had not time to feel! Bequest of darkness, yet of light, since unborne by him. "Where thou goest, *we* will go" — how mutual, how intimate! No solitude receives him, but neighborhood and friend.

Relieved forever of the loss of those that must have fled, but for his sweet haste. Knowing he could not spare *them,* he hurried like a boy from that unhappened sorrow. Death has mislaid his sting — the grave forgot his victory. Because the flake fell not on him, we will accept the drift, and wade where he is lain.

Do you remember the clover leaf? The little hand that plucked it will keep tight hold of mine.

Please give her love to Annie, and Kate, who also gave a father.

Emily.

Later in the month Mrs. Holland sent Emily some of the numerous obituary articles which appeared in the papers after Dr. Holland's death. The New York evening papers had made the announcement the same day, and the following day, or in later issues, the papers in New York, Boston, Philadelphia, Chicago, St. Louis, and many smaller towns carried editorials about him, in some of which his death was linked with that of President Garfield, three weeks before. Dr. Holland himself had been deeply affected by the President's death, and his last published work was a sonnet on the subject, printed in the *New York Tribune.* On the day before he died he was writing an editorial about Garfield for *The Century,* and said of him, "His sympathy for the humble drew to him the hearts of the world." His friends remarked that he might have been writing his own epitaph.

Letters and personal testimonials from persons in many states were printed in the papers, and memorial articles appeared in a number of periodicals, in England and Canada, as well as in his own country. Many of them spoke of his founding of *Scribner's Monthly* as his greatest contribution to American life. In the fortnightly literary periodical, *The Critic,* published in New York, the twenty-second of October 1881, there was a biographical article beginning with the following paragraphs, which in their unbiased evaluation may best be used here to sum up the general opinion of those who understood Dr. Holland's relation to the people of his own time.

> The suddenness of Dr. Holland's death was startling. He died when death was farthest from his thoughts, though he had known for years that the end would come unexpectedly. The news spread with singular rapidity among his friends, of whom there was not one but felt the shock of a personal bereavement. Dr. Holland's popularity was of such a character that thousands even of those who had never seen him had come to regard him as a friend and counsellor.
>
> Perhaps no man in this country has helped so many persons on their path of life by written or spoken works of kindness and wise advice. If he preached in his stories and poems, as well as in his ostensibly didactic writings, it was because he was born a preacher, and had an unfailing spirit of sympathy and helpfulness. There was nothing in him of cant or bigotry, and while he was himself a good deal of a conservative in religious opinions, he allowed a wide latitude to others. He believed in character rather than in creed. The elements of his popularity may be analyzed some other time; at present it is only necessary that their potency should be confessed. There have been greater writers in America than Dr. Holland; men of greater force, of broader scope, of higher cultivation have survived him; but there has been none of purer aims or wider influence. And if the quality of his literary work was not always of the highest, the readers of his longer poems and his later novels have been struck by many passages that showed an artist's hand, while some of his shorter

poems are worthy of preservation in every collection of the best American verse. As a moralist, however, he made his deepest mark; and for their moral teachings his books will continue to be read.

LXVII

[Late October 1881]

Sister.

I wanted to read the dear Articles slowly – one by one – and alone – as under the circumstances each one of them seemed an interview with the Departed – but that was unpermitted – so I snatched a Line at a time – taking it with me as I worked, and then returning for another.

Each is true – and more – and so warmly lifelike, it almost gives a diffidence, like admiration of a friend in his tender presence.

I have rarely seen so sincere a modesty on a mature Cheek as on Dr Holland's – and one almost feels an intrusiveness in proclaiming him, lest it profane his simplicity.

It was nearly Morning, last Night, when I went to my Room from the loved perusal, and when I laid it in the Drawer, the Telegram of the Heavenly Flight was close beside without design.

It shall always remain there – nearest us – in the Room to the East Father loved the most, and where I bade the Doctor Good Night, that November Morning – He put one Hand on Vinnie's Head and the other on mine*, and his Heart on your's, as we both knew, and said that the Sunshine and the Scene he should always remember.

* First written *your's*: erased.

No Autumn's intercepting Chill
Appalls that Tropic Breast –
But African Exuberance
And Asiatic Rest.

Poor "Little Child Wife"!

Lovingly,

Emily.

The plans for Annie's marriage to John Howe were carried out in spite of the recent death of her father, and the wedding took place on Theodore's birthday, the seventh of December 1881. Dr. Holland had been deeply interested in her approaching marriage, as his friends knew. Emily's friend, Helen Hunt Jackson, a frequent contributor to *Scribner's Monthly,* alluded to this in the opening lines of a poem written on the day of his death and published in the December number of the *Century* (the second stanza is here omitted).

We may not choose! Ah, if we might, how we
Should linger here, not ready to be dead,
Till one more loving thing were looked or said –
Till some dear child's estate of joy should be
Complete – or we, triumphant, late, should see
Some great cause win, for which our hearts had bled –
Some hope come true which all our lives had fed –
Some bitter sorrow fade away and flee,
Which we, rebellious, had too bitter thought;
Or even, so our human hearts would cling,
If but they might, to this fair world inwrought
With heavenly beauty in each smallest thing –
We would refuse to die till we had sought
One violet more, heard one more robin sing!

Emily, seeing farther and deeper, was able to touch every aspect of the meaning of the day when she wrote in response to Mrs. Holland's account of the wedding.

LXVIII

[Mid-December 1881]

Sweet Sister, – We were much relieved to know that the dear event had occurred without overwhelming any loved one, and perhaps it is sweeter and safer so. I feared much for the parting, to you, to whom parting has come so thickly in the last few days. I knew all would be beautiful, and rejoice it was. Few daughters have the immortality of a father for a bridal gift. Could there be one more costly?

As we never have ceased to think of you, we will more tenderly, now. Confide our happiness to Annie, in her happiness. We hope the unknown balm may ease the balm withdrawn.

You and Katie, the little sisters, lose her, yet obtain her, for each new width of love largens all the rest. Mother and Vinnie think and speak. Vinnie hopes to write. Would that mother could, but her poor hand is idle. Shall I return to you your last and sweetest words – "But I love you all"?

Emily.

As she had done at every Christmas season for so many years, Mrs. Holland sent her usual gift to the friends at Amherst. Her life was sturdily carried on, in spite of the empty place at its center. Since Annie, now married, had moved away, and Ted was a senior at Yale, only Kate remained at home with her, and the two were drawn more closely together.

The package had arrived early, and, deeply touched by her friend's thoughtfulness in the time of her mourning, Emily wrote to her tenderly before Christmas Day had come.

LXIX

[Before Christmas 1881]

Dare we wish the brave sister a sweet Christmas, who remembered us punctually in sorrow as in peace?

The broken heart is broadest. Had it come all the way in your little hand, it could not have reached us perfecter, though had it, we should have clutched the hand and forgot the rest.

Fearing the day had associations of anguish to you, I was just writing when your token came. Then, humbled with wonder at your self-forgetting, I delayed till now. Reminded again of gigantic Emily Brontë, of whom her Charlotte said "Full of ruth for others, on herself she had no mercy." The hearts that never lean, must fall. To moan is justified.

To thank you for remembering under the piercing circumstances were a profanation.

God bless the hearts that suppose they are beating and are not, and enfold in His infinite tenderness those that do not know they are beating and are.

Shall we wish a triumphant Christmas to the brother withdrawn? Certainly he possesses it.

> How much of Source escapes with thee —
> How chief thy sessions be —
> For thou has borne a universe
> Entirely away.

With wondering love.

Emily.

"Whom seeing not, we" clasp.

Emily.

Always deeply moved by the sorrows of her friends, Emily often shared with them through her poetry the thoughts that she felt might bring them comfort. Such a poem is this one, written as a letter, and probably sent within a few months after Dr. Holland's death.

LXX

[Late 1881?]

Dear Sister.

The Things that never can come back, are several –
Childhood – some forms of Hope – the Dead –
Though Joys – like Men – may sometimes make a Journey –
And still abide.
We do not mourn for Traveler, or Sailor,
Their Routes are fair –
But think enlarged of all that they will tell us
Returning here.
"Here!" There are typic "Heres" –
Foretold Locations –
The Spirit does not stand –
Himself – at whatsoever Fathom
His Native Land.

Emily, in love –

PART FIVE

1882–1886

The circle of those who were close to Emily Dickinson was diminishing. Her father, Mr. Bowles, Dr. Holland — three men, diverse in character and outlook, each of whom held special meaning for her — were gone. Her way of life made her peculiarly vulnerable; each loss she suffered diminished her world to the full extent of that person's value to her. Now a new blow came that struck still deeper into her life.

On the first of April 1882, the Reverend Charles Wadsworth died. We cannot know the exact nature of the relation between them, even if we would, for no written words contain the story, and it is plain that Emily's own sister did not understand it. To fit it into the pattern of what the world calls a "love affair" is to disregard the terms in which Emily herself wrote of it, and to identify Dr. Wadsworth with the "atom" she "preferred" is to be dangerously specific. The place held by any one individual in the life of so sensitive a person cannot be fully understood except in relation to all the other factors in her emotional growth, and this involves an intrusion that her reticence precludes. Not until the poems have been dated and arranged in chronological order will the pattern of her inner life emerge, and even then it will be the reflection of a soul's evolution rather than a chronicle of personal relationships.

Of Dr. Wadsworth's preëminent importance to her, however, over a period embracing the whole of her adult life, there is no doubt, for her own words clearly reveal her feeling. What other values he may have held for her beyond those of counselor and dearest friend, to which she gave him title in writing of him after his death, we can only guess. At the time of their first meeting, Dr. Wadsworth, who was already prominent as a clergyman, was a married man seventeen years her senior. When he died at sixty-eight, revered and worn by years of service, he was survived by his wife and three children. If this had been a story of mutual passion and renunciation, the correspondence that continued until his death would not have been consistent with his known character and attitude toward life, nor would it have been in keeping with Dr. and Mrs. Holland's views to forward love letters to a married man. Emily would not have betrayed their confidence by asking them to do so.

If the attachment was not of a passionate nature, neither can it be explained as the one-sided adoration of a young girl for an older man to whom she has projected the qualities of a God whom theology has failed to reveal to her. Though her feeling may have held such an element at first, an illusion would not have sufficed as a basis for a lifetime devotion for a woman of Emily's depth; there must have been a unique value in the relationship on both sides, strong enough to stand the test of years, and deepening with experience. To Emily, Dr. Wadsworth seemed the embodiment of all that was most clear and sure in the Christian faith, yet she has suggested that he was torn by a hidden conflict when she wrote of him to Mr. Clark as "a dusk gem, born of troubled waters." It is conceivable that the part of him that found no place in his conception of the life to which he was pledged was reflected in Emily in a living form he could accept and in which he could find release. The enduring friendship which Emily counted as her greatest earthly treasure may have grown to such depth and fertility precisely because it was not invested with the quality she described as "the infinite aurora," but with a rare and genuine understanding.

No third person can adequately interpret so subtle a relationship, yet ambiguous as it may appear, we should remember that its form was not inconsistent with the conventions of Emily's own generation, which, even though they did not bind her spirit, were a part of her social background. Those conventions—based as they were on a morality that separated "carnal" from "spiritual" love—left the way open for an astonishing degree of freedom in friendship between men and women of fine feeling.

The great loss Emily suffered in the death of one "whom to know was life," with those that preceded and others that followed, made an irreparable breach in her world; but the stripping away of personal attachments did not lessen her interest in human experience. The letters of her last years are the expression of a free and ripe personality for whom life had taken on a new simplicity as her individual demands upon it were relinquished.

We do not know whether, after Dr. Wadsworth's death, Emily wrote to Mrs. Holland about this dear friend to whom she had forwarded so many letters. There is none now remaining that was written during the first six months, but several that follow allude to her loss in a way that seems to assume Mrs. Holland would understand its significance. Events that concerned Mrs. Holland herself were the occasion of the next letter, written the following autumn.

In the spring of 1882, Kate Holland became engaged to Bleecker Van Wagenen of New York and was married to him the twenty-seventh of the following September. Less prompt than usual in response to events in her friends' lives, Emily let more than a month pass before she wrote to congratulate them. While she was writing, the news came that Mrs. Holland's brother, Charles O. Chapin of Springfield, had died suddenly on the twenty-eighth of October in the State House at Boston, where he was acting as a member of the Massachusetts Prison Commission. As a friend of Samuel Bowles, he had been entertained at Austin Dickinson's house, but it seems to have been in connection with one of her early visits to Springfield that Emily remembered him. In writing now she does not send the congratulatory note, but a letter of sympathy instead. She alludes to special associations of gain or loss connected with certain months, and while it is difficult to trace the repeated instances of which she speaks, the feeling of loss she associates with April is sufficiently accounted for by the death of Dr. Wadsworth, only half a year before.

LXXI

[29? October 1882]

Dear Sister.

You knew we would come as soon as we knew — The little Group at the Springfield Table has indeed diminished —

Doctor – Mother – Brother. I am glad I have seen your noble Brother, for now I can miss him from Affection rather than report. Like my Father he went to Boston to die. All who die in Boston are endeared to me — 'Twas his Isle of flight.

I was just writing you in congratulatory gladness, when the dark words came. I hope it is not too much for your dear – Over burdened Spirit. October could not pass you by.

It sometimes seems as if special Months gave and took away.

August has brought the most to me – April – robbed me most – in incessant instances.

Your Brother bore a strong resemblance to a Childhood's friend who long since died, and whose look I never have seen repeated.

It is almost involuntary with me to send my Note to that Home in the Grass where your many lie.

Could I visit the Beds of my own who sleep, as reprovelessly, even Night were sweet.

With tender thought of Kate in her joyful Hour.

Emily.

It was scarcely more than two weeks later that the mother whom Emily and Lavinia had nursed with such devotion reached the end of her seven long years of invalidism. Emily Norcross Dickinson died the fourteenth of November 1882, at the age of seventy-eight. Emily's tender solicitude followed her into death and beyond, as if she were a lost child. She wrote to the Norcross cousins, "I had hoped to write you before, but Mother's dying almost stunned my spirit. I have answered a few inquiries of love, but written little intuitively" (*Letters*, p. 267).

In this letter to Mrs. Holland, written while the immediate event still blotted out all else, she answers one of the "inquiries of love."

ANNIE AND KATE HOLLAND

LAVINIA DICKINSON · 1896

LXXII

[Mid-November 1882]

The dear Mother that could not walk, has *flown*. It never occurred to us that though she had not Limbs, she had *Wings* – and she soared from us unexpectedly as a summoned Bird. She had a few weeks since a violent cold, though so had we all, but our's recovered apparently, her's seemed more reluctant – but her trusted Physician was with her, who returned her to us so many times when she thought to go, and he felt no alarm. After her cough ceased she suffered much from neuralgic pain, which as nearly as we can know, committed the last wrong. She seemed entirely better the last Day of her Life and took Lemonade – Beef Tea and Custard with a pretty ravenousness that delighted us. After a restless Night, complaining of great weariness, she was lifted earlier than usual from her Bed to her Chair, when a few quick breaths and a "Dont leave me, Vinnie" and her sweet being closed. That the one we have cherished so softly so long, should be in that great Eternity without our simple Counsels, seems frightened and foreign, but we hope that Our Sparrow has ceased to fall, though at first we believe nothing.

Thank you for the Love – I was sure whenever I lost my own I should find your Hand.

The Clover you brought me from Father's Grave, Spring will sow on Mother's – and she carried Violets in her Hand to encourage her.

Remember me to your Annie and Kate. Tell them I envy them their Mother. "Mother"! What a Name!

Emily.

Emily had begun to feel the strangeness of her mother's absence, and the loneliness had become more acute when she wrote again. She was now fully aware of the quality of her relation to her mother, which had changed its character during the years of Mrs. Dickinson's illness. At about the same time she wrote to the Misses Norcross: "The great mission of pain had been ratified – cultivated to tenderness by a persistent sorrow, so that a larger mother died than had she died before" (*Letters*, p. 267).

The following letter went to a new address, for Mrs. Holland had sold her Park Avenue house in October 1882, when she and Theodore went to live with the Van Wagenens, who had taken a house on East Thirty-fourth Street. Mrs. Holland made her home with them for the rest of her life, but in the summers she continued to be hostess to her enlarging family circle at Bonniecastle. The new circumstances in her friend's life were made vivid to Emily through an account her brother Austin gave her of a call he made on the family at their New York home.

LXXIII

[19? December 1882]

Dear Sister.

I have thought of you with confiding Love, but to speak seemed taken from me. Blow has followed blow, till the wondering terror of the Mind clutches what is left, helpless of an accent.

Your have spared so much and so patiently, it seems as if some seraphic Armor must have shielded you.

Mother has now been gone five Weeks. We should have thought it a long Visit, were she coming back. Now the "Forever" thought almost shortens it, as we are nearer rejoining her than her own return. We were never intimate Mother and Children while she was our Mother – but Mines in the same

Ground meet by tunneling and when she became our Child, the Affection came. When we were Children and she journeyed, she always brought us something. Now, would she bring us but herself, what an only Gift. Memory is a strange Bell – Jubilee, and Knell.

I hope your Home with the new Children is a Place of Peace, and believe it to be from Austin's Story. The Port of Peace has many Coves, though the main entrance cease. I hope the large sons are docile to their little Mother, whose commands are Balm. I had written to Kate, but ere mailing the Note that great difference came, and to find it would be to open a Past that is safer closed.

Austin told of his Call with much warmth, and I trust the Sun is still shining there, though it is since Night.

I trust the new Home may remain untouched. Is God Love's Adversary?

Emily.

Mrs. Holland remembered the absent mother in the message that came with her usual Christmas gift, and in thanking her for it Emily recalled how her mother's bedside had been the center of the family life.

This letter appears at first sight to consist of two incomplete fragments. The two sheets of paper are of different kinds, and the absence of punctuation at the end of the first gives the impression that the words form an unfinished sentence ("Santa Claus, though *illustrates* – Revelation"), while the second begins with a new sentence. A thread of meaning, however, may be traced between them, and since one kind of paper was used in some of the preceding letters and the other in the one that follows, they may quite easily have been the last in one box and the first in another. Emily made a similar use of two papers in a later letter (LXXXVI). The tone is entirely consistent in the two halves, and two points in the content of the second indicate that it was written at the same time as the first. Austin's call on the family in New York is again mentioned, and an allusion to Maggie suggests that she also had been remembered in the Christmas package.

LXXIV

[After Christmas 1882]

Sweet Sister.

The lovely recollection – the thought of those that cannot "taste" – of one to whose faint Bed all Boons were brought before revealed, made the sweet Package mighty. It came so long it knows the way and almost comes itself, like Nature's faithful Blossoms whom no one summons but themselves, Magics of Constancy.

The Fiction of "Santa Claus" always reminds me of the reply to my early question of "Who made the Bible" — "Holy Men moved by the Holy Ghost," and though I have now ceased my investigations, the Solution is insufficient.

Santa Claus, though *illustrates*. Revelation

But a Book is only the Heart's Portrait – every Page a Pulse.

Thank you for the protecting words. The petit Shepherd would find us but a startled Flock, not an unloving one.

Remember me to your Possessions, in whom I have a tender claim, and take sweet care of the small Life, fervor has made great – deathless as Emerson's "Squirrel."

Vinnie gives her love and will write, if a Lady goes away who is calling here. Maggie prized your remembrance. Austin seldom calls. I am glad you were glad to see him. He visits rarely as Gabriel.

Lovingly,

Emily.

The emptiness of a house from which the carefully tended life that formed the center of its activity has been withdrawn echoes in Emily's next letter. Her reticence seldom allowed her to express the acute pain of her sorrow, which is heard here almost as an involuntary cry torn from her while she wrote. All her losses are now gathered into one, and she has come to identify the date of Dr. Wadsworth's death, the first of April, with the death of all the loved.

But it was not Emily's intention to burden her friend, and as usual she was full of sympathetic interest in the events of concern to the Hollands. Sometime during January or February Kate went south with her husband, who was obliged to take a business trip. While there Bleecker Van Wagenen, whose name was a stumbling block Emily tried to avoid, was taken ill, and the bride who had accompanied him in holiday mood was obliged to take responsibility for his care in a strange town.

Meanwhile, in New York, it seems that Mrs. Holland was again having trouble with her eyes, though Emily's allusion to it, as in an earlier letter, through Mrs. Browning's poem on Caterina and her lover Camoens, is made confusing by her spelling of the name *Katrina* – a variation suggestive of Kate.

This is the first in a series of five related letters written between January and the end of March, the sequence of which can be fitted together only by inference, since only one can be accurately dated. The flavor of Christmas that still hangs over the first, with two chocolate drops still remaining in the box Mrs. Holland had sent, appears inconsistent with the date of the Van Wagenens' southern trip, which is mentioned again as having recently occurred in the definitely dated letter of the third of March. While not entirely convincing, the present arrangement is the best I have been able to make with the limited information I possess.

LXXV

[Early 1883]

Dear friend,

We were very sorrowful for the illness of the Gentleman with the long Name, and it must have been a bleak Holiday for your loved Kate – Would it be chivalrous to say, we rejoice it was "Bleeker"? And for Katrina's Eyes, Camoens is sorry.

We hope "Mr-Bridegroom" is better, as Gilbert calls those sacred ones, and that the Eyes relent – May it not be the glazed Light which the Snows make, for with us they are falling always now, and the last is faithful for three Days, an inclement constancy.

Could I thank you for all the sweetness at once, it would deprive me of the joy of thanking you again, which I so much covet. Of the Christmas Munificence two Acorns remain – Those I shall save for Seed, and I know they will bloom by another Christmas. Mother's Christmas Gift of another Life is just as stupendous to us now as the Morning it came – All other Surprise is at last monotonous, but the Death of the Loved is all moments – *now*. Love has but one Date – "The first of April" "Today, Yesterday, and Forever."

"*Can* Trouble dwell with April Days?"
"Of Love that never found it's earthly close,
what sequel?"

Both in the same Book – in the same Hymn. Excuse your Mourning Emily.

Austin Dickinson's report of his call on the Hollands remained with Emily all winter, building for her in imagination a picture of them and their home. For the third time she referred to it in the next letter, in which we learn that Austin had given her a description of Ted, who had graduated from Yale in June 1882 and was now living at home while attending the law school of Columbia University. Proud of her son, and pleased with her sons-in-law, Mrs. Holland sent photographs of the three young men, so that Emily and Vinnie might see for themselves how they looked.

LXXVI

[Early 1883]

Dear Sister.

Thank you for the glimpse. The Faces are delightful –

Had I imagined Annie's friend, he looks as I believed.

The other two surprised me – Ted's, by the boyishness.

I looked for an Octogenarian flavor in a Graduate – and perhaps Austin's assurance that he wore the Supreme Court Judge's Coat, aided the delusion. The Eyes are the Father's – though why so stealthy – but the Mother's Mouth. Where to flatter is truth, what respite for flattery? The other Face is deep and sweet, a lovely Face to sit by in Life's Mysterious Boat.

I hope the missing Health is rapidly returning – and grieve that any faintness should waste your second Home.

It acclimates our thought of you to see your Noble Sons.

If the Spirits are fair as the Faces "Nothing is here for Tears."

May I present your Portrait to your Sons in Law?

To see her is a Picture –
To hear her is a Tune –
To know her an Intemperance
As innocent as June –
To know her not – Affliction –
To own her for a Friend
A warmth as near as if the Sun
Were shining in your Hand.

Emily.

The Van Wagenens, now back from their disastrous southern trip, were doubtless pleased with Emily's comment on Bleecker's picture, as Mrs. Holland must have been with the little poem. One can imagine that the gentleman – whose name Emily attempted to write this time but sadly misspelled – suggested that his wife's picture should also be sent. The "suggester" and the "enacter" of the plan, to whom Emily sends thanks, were obviously others than Mrs. Holland herself, and it was probably Kate who sent at her husband's request the photograph of herself and her sister which Emily describes. We may infer from the letter that Mrs. Holland, to whom Emily refers as "the ill Linnet," was suffering from an attack of rheumatism, to which she was becoming increasingly subject.

LXXVII

[3 March 1883]

Were not the Faces too lovely, I should say the remembrance were lovelier, but a perilous Chivalry being involved, I regard the limitude.

Annie looks the pathetic Squirrel that she always was and Kate a questioning Dove.

Her question however is answered now. Please tell her from me.

> The Clock strikes one that just struck two –
> Some schism in the Sum –
> A Vagabond from Genesis
> Has wrecked the Pendulum.

The instant acquiescence was delightfully hearty – the suddenness of a tenderness making it more sweet.

Thank the Suggester and the Enacter, and once more, please, a little news of the ill Linnet.

We trust Mr-Van Wagner retakes his fleeing Health. Should suggest a Policeman, and that Kate found Flowers and wonder in the Sweet Land.

March is three Days with me, but his Face is so unbecoming still, I dont show him to Strangers.

With love for each, and a shy smile at the new Brethren,

Emily –

After Emily's letter of the third of March had been received by her friends in New York, the mail carried back to her two separate items which she received at different times, because one of them went astray. Her misspelling of "Van Wagenen" brought a prompt response, to which she refers as a reprimand, probably from Kate, to whom she sends an apology in the next letter. In reading it, Mrs. Holland would have remembered Emily's habit of putting her own words into the mouths of others, and would not have been deceived by the guileless fiction of the clergyman to whom she attributes the confusion she probably felt as a child listening to the words she heard from the pulpit.

The second item in the mail – a letter or package which Emily calls simply "The Birds" – must have come from Mrs. Holland herself, for Emily's letter beginning "Dear friends" shows that more than one person was involved. While it is possible that the "Birds" had no connection with the photographs that played such a large part in the rapid sequence of letters, but referred to a book or some other gift Mrs. Holland had sent, Emily's use of quotation marks suggests that the word was first used by Mrs. Holland herself, and that she had written again on the subject of the photograph, which showed the girls sitting side by side with their heads tilted together. Emily might have returned it with her last letter, assuming that it was a loan – as seems to have been the case with the photographs of the three men – and perhaps Mrs. Holland sent it back, saying that it was intended for a present. In the letter that accompanied it she might have objected to Emily's description of Annie as a "pathetic squirrel" while Kate was compared to a dove, and declared that *both* her daughters should be likened to birds.

Another piece of family news that Mrs. Holland's letter contained was that Annie and her husband, John Howe, were about to start on a European tour lasting several months. The biblical phrase Emily used in alluding to the coming voyage could have had a literal meaning, for Annie was a poor sailor, and John probably announced that he would keep her walking the deck all the way across.

LXXVIII

[March 1883]

Dear friends.

The "Birds" preceded the *Reprimand,* which modified it's chastening.

By some divine contingency that strayed to Austin's Box, which deferred it's rancor till fortified by Birds, we had grown impervious.

Orthography always baffled me, and to "Ns" I had an especial aversion, as they always seemed unfinished *M's.* Will dear

Mrs "Van Wagenen" excuse me for taking her portentous name in vain?

I can best express my contrition in the words of the Prayer of a Clergyman I heard when a Child – "Oh thou who sittest upon the Apex of the Cherubim, look down upon this, thine unworthy Terrapin"!

The dear Birds and their Donor will accept our love for the untiring Sweetness. To never forget to be gracious is Remembrance' most touching Ornament.

The Health that omits to mention itself, we trust is so culpable only because it is better, and hope that Annie's Walk on the Water was a pedestrian success.

With memory for each, what sweeter Shelter than the Hearts of such a hallowed Household!

Emily.

The month of March, with its varying moods of roughness alternating with the tender promise of spring, seemed always to bring new vitality to Emily's spirit, and her imagination was captured by it as by an undisciplined but colorful personality. Ever concerned over the health of her friend, she wrote for the third time during the month to inquire for Mrs. Holland's rheumatism, and to send a poem announcing the arrival of the robins. Since Mrs. Holland had written earlier in the winter of having trouble with her eyes, she had probably accepted the services of her daughter or a niece who was sometimes with her to take down her letters from dictation, but Emily slyly pleads this time for a few words written with her own hand, to reassure her that the health which omitted "to mention itself" in the last letter was really improving.

LXXIX

[March 1883]

We wont fatigue the Fairy Scribe with a farther Letter, but only ask that question small, ever to us so great – how is the Mama? We hope the March Winds may not find her in her dear Retreat, for their ferocious ways would certainly appall her.

We trust the lovely Invalid is growing every Day, not in Grace but Vigor, the latter Foliage needed more.

I have seen one Bird and part of another – probably the last, for Gibraltar's Feathers would be dismayed by this Savage Air – beautiful, too, ensnaring – as Spring always is.

"Though he slay me, yet will I trust him."

Commending the Birds of which I spoke, to your Hearts and Crumbs,

Lovingly,

Emily.

Forever honored be the Tree
Whose Apple Winterworn
Enticed to Breakfast from the Sky
Two Gabriels Yestermorn.

They registered in Nature's Book
As Robins –Sire and Son –
But Angels have that modest way
To screen them from Renown.

When Mrs. Holland wrote next it was with her own hand, and Emily was touchingly grateful for the feeling of closeness the note brought to her. There was news in it, which remains unexplained, of some younger person who was meeting her first sorrow, but it also contained the good news that Kate was expecting a baby. When Emily answered she wrote understandingly of the adjustments Mrs. Holland had been obliged to make in giving up her home and turning over her responsibilities to the younger generation.

LXXX

[Spring 1883]

It was sweet to touch the familiar Hand that so long had led us. "Though thou walk through the Valley of the Shadow of Death, I will be with thee," you have taught us was no Exaggeration. How many times we have each crossed it, would either of us dare to count, but we must bring no Twilight to one who lost her Dawn.

It is very dear you are better. You have had much struggle. That is the deepest illness.

The Birds are very bold this Morning, and sing without a Crumb. "Meat that we know not of," perhaps, slily handed them. I used to spell the one of that name "*Fee Bee*" when a Child, and have seen no need to improve! Should I spell all the things as they sounded to me, and say all the facts as I saw them, it would send consternation among more than the "*Fee Bees*"!

Vinnie picked the Sub rosas, and handed them to me, in your wily Note.

Kisses for "Brooks of Sheffield." Am glad Annie is well, and that Kate is sacred. Tell her with my love, "I give my Angels charge." For the sweet Founder of the Fold, the bereft Madonna, more love than "we can ask or think" –

Emily.

Emily seems to have followed the announcements of coming publications and to have read the new books that interested her as soon as they were out. When a book concerned a person to whom she was strongly drawn she waited for it with special eagerness. Such a book was the biography of Emily Brontë by A. Mary F. Robinson, one of Roberts Brothers' *Famous Women Series*, which was published the fifteenth of April 1883. Since up to that time the only available accounts of Emily Brontë's life had been a few articles in magazines or the incidental one contained in Mrs. Gaskell's *Life of Charlotte Brontë*, Emily lost no time in obtaining the book. Before the middle of May, she had read it and found it so affecting that she wrote and urged Mrs. Holland to make the effort it would cost her to try to read it. Mrs. Holland probably did read it, or had it read aloud to her, for a copy of the book, which was among those the family owned at that time, is still in my possession.

When Emily wrote this letter she was expecting daily to hear of the death of her cousin William Hawley Dickinson of Worcester, the son of her father's brother William. In earlier years, Emily and Lavinia had been especially fond of this cousin of about their own age, who had been one of their chosen group while he was a student at Amherst. He died the fifteenth of May 1883. Writing a few days before this event, Emily questions whether Mrs. Holland already had carried out a plan she had mentioned of leaving New York as soon as the spring weather became agreeable. She would hardly have gone so early to Alexandria Bay, but might have been planning to make some visits before settling for the season at her summer home.

LXXXI

[Early May 1883]

Sister.

I received a Card a few Days since, saying that "as soon as the Weather permitted," you would not be there. Has the Weather yet made those Advances? Not knowing where the

Dear Ones are, I must cherish them heterogeniously till farther notice.

Loving the Blest without Abode, this too can be learned.

I wish the dear Eyes would so far relent as to let you read "Emily Bronte" – more electric far than anything since "Jane Eyre."

Napoleon of the Cross! Try and read a few lines at a time – and then a few more later. It is so so strange a Strength, I must have you possess it. Our Cousin, Willie Dickinson, is dying at Saratoga, and the stricken Letters of his Wife reach us every Mail.

We have written to Willie not to be homesick because his Mother and our Father would'nt have stayed so long if it were not a lovely place. How deep this Lifetime is – One guess at the Waters, and we are plunged beneath!

I send to your New York Home, hoping if you have fled, the Note may pursue you through some of Love's Deputies, and am Emily, with Vinnie's affection, and Maggie's "respects."

There is an interval of several months before the date of the next letter, written late in September. Emily may have written others during the summer, but if so she had failed to mention until now the sympathetic interest she felt in an item she had read in the *Springfield Republican* of the tenth of July. It told of the completion of a monument to Dr. Holland in the Springfield cemetery, with the placing of a bronze portrait in bas-relief by Augustus Saint-Gaudens. On the granite base of the monument were inscribed the characteristic words with which he closed his will: "For the great hereafter I trust in the infinite love, as it is expressed to me in the life and death of my Lord and Savior Jesus Christ."

Two other events of importance to Mrs. Holland had occurred, to which Emily's letter alludes. The first took place at Bonniecastle, where on the eighth of August her first grandchild, Kathrina Holland Van Wagenen, was born. If the baby had been a boy, he would have been named for his grandfather Holland. The little girl bore instead the name of the heroine of his popular poem, *Kathrina.* A month later Mrs. Holland's happiness was clouded by the death of her younger sister whom Emily remembered as "Minnie." Amelia Chapin May died on the ninth of September, and a notice was sent to the *Springfield Republican,* in which Vinnie, if not Emily herself, would have been expected to see it, but the news did not reach Emily until she heard it from Mrs. Holland a week or two later. In three successive years Mrs. Holland had lost her husband, her brother, and her sister, and in writing of this latest sorrow Emily was caught by the sudden fear that her friend might follow them.

An allusion to an experience of Ted's of which his mother had written suggests that he had recently had an encounter with royal personages. It seems probable that the occasion was at the Canadian industrial fair at Toronto which was opened by the Marquis of Lorne, the retiring governor-general, and his wife, Princess Louise, on the twelfth of September. It was an easy journey overnight by boat from Alexandria Bay to Toronto, and the fair must have attracted many American visitors.

LXXXII

[Late September 1883]

Dear One.

No one had told me your Sister had died. I sweetly remember her on my first Visit to you – a tender-timid face, with the appealing look that the ones have, who do not hear entirely.

Perhaps the Brother called her.

"The Kingdom and the Power" may not have filled a Sister's place. For this new solitude to you I am freshly grieved. Would that a few familiar Lips might be left to you, now the best have stopped!

We read with deep affection of the dear Doctor's Emblem – in the Republican – proud that each farthest reach of Love had been ratified. I hope he thinks of us. I am glad you are in the open Air. That is nearest Heaven.

The first Abode "not made with Hands" entices to the second.

I have thought of you with peculiar urgency for the last few days.

Can it be there was cause?

Said a rude but wondering Mind to me, a Carpenter at work here, "I cant tell how it is, but there *are* influences."

Even my Puritan Spirit "gangs" sometimes "aglay."

Sweetest Love for Kate, and Annie when you see her, and say with "Heathcliff" to little Katrina – "Oh Cathie – Cathie!"

Theodore probably witnessed nothing so "royal" as himself, of which with warm remembrance convince him. Vinnie gives her Heart and Maggie her love, though how do the gifts vary? And I, consign myself to you and find the Nest sufficient. Take faithful care of the dear health and flee no sudden day from your dependent

Emily.

It could hardly have been more than a week after Emily had written the last letter that her beloved little nephew Gilbert was taken ill, and after a few days of uncontrollable fever, died on the fifth of October. Emily's grief at this overwhelming blow – the loss of the precious child who had been the source of her greatest joy during the few years of his life – wrenched her spirit so severely that she was prostrated. It was not until January that she was able to return to normal living, and though she carried on her accustomed routine through the rest of that winter and spring, her vitality had been so seriously drained that she never fully recovered the normal balance of her health. It seems to have been during her illness that she wrote this letter to Mrs. Holland.

LXXXIII

[November? 1883]

Sweet Sister.

Was that what I used to call you?

I hardly recollect, all seems so different.

I hesitate which word to take, as I can take but few and each must be the chiefest, but recall that Earth's most graphic transaction is placed within a syllable, nay, even a gaze.

The Physician says I have "Nervous prostration."

Possibly I have – I do not know the Names of Sickness. The Crisis of the sorrow of so many years is all that tires me. As Emily Bronte to her Maker, I write to my Lost "Every Existence would exist in thee."

The tender consternation for you was much eased by the little Card, which spoke "*better*" as loud as a human Voice.

Please, Sister, to wait.

"Open the Door, open the Door, they are waiting for me," was Gilbert's sweet command in delirium. *Who* were waiting for him, all we possess we would give to know. Anguish at last opened it, and he ran to the little Grave at his Grandparents' feet. All this and more, though *is* there more? More than Love and Death? Then tell me it's name!

Love for the sweet Catharines, Rose and Bud in one, and the Gentleman with the vast Name, and Annie and Ted, and if the softest for yourself, would they ever know, or knowing, covet?

How lovely that you went to "Church"!
May I go with you to the "Church of the first born?"

Emily.

In the preceding letter Emily expressed consternation over Mrs. Holland's health, yet, so far as I am aware, she did not suffer from any serious or prolonged illness. Her occasional attacks of rheumatism were certainly painful, but Emily's solicitude was probably more acute than the facts warranted because of her own growing sense of living in a dissolving world. Mrs. Holland was actively participating in the life of her home, and in the course of the winter she wrote with enthusiam about her grandchild. Emily's reply suggests that she might find cause for jealousy.

The impression of early spring which the letter gives through its description of flowers indoors and birds outdoors is misleading, for the sequence of letters that follow makes it probable that this one was written in late January or early February. Blue jays are winter residents in Massachusetts, and Emily wrote only of having planted hyacinths, not of their being in bloom. Carnations bloom earlier, as she implies in a letter to Maria Whitney, written the same winter (*Letters*, p. 335): "There are scarlet carnations, with a witching suggestion, and hyacinths covered with promises which I know they will keep."

LXXXIV

[Early 1884]

Sweet Sister.

The contemplation of you as "Grandma" is a touching novelty to which the Mind adjusts itself by reverent degrees.

That nothing in her Life became her like it's last event, it is probable. So the little Engrosser has done her work, and Love's "remainder Biscuit" is henceforth for us.

We will try to bear it as divinely as Othello did, who had he had Love's sweetest slice, would not have charmed the World.

Austin heard Salvini before his Idol died, and the size of that manifestation even the Grave has not foreclosed.

I saw the Jays this Morning, each in a Blue Pelisse, and would have kissed their Lips of Horn, if I could have caught them, but Nature took good care!

I have made a permanent Rainbow by filling a Window with Hyacinths, which Science will be glad to know, and have a Cargo of Carnations, worthy of Ceylon, but Science and Ceylon are Strangers to me, and I would give them both for one look of the gone Eyes, glowing in Paradise. There are too many to count, now, and I measure by Fathoms, Numbers past away.

With longings for the sweet Health and Seraphic Peace of my little Sister,

Her Lover,

Emily.

In the interval between the last letter and the one that follows, Mrs. Holland had been away, probably on a visit in Springfield or Northampton, where she had an unexpected encounter with Lavinia, from whom Emily received an account of the episode. The circumstances under which they met gave an atmosphere of high adventure to Lavinia's recital of the story, but the clues to what actually occurred are too indistinct for us to follow.

Mrs. Holland had written of another and less agreeable adventure that had overtaken the family in the house on Thirty-fourth Street. They were driven out in the middle of the night by a clogged sewer which "backed up" in the cellar, and were forced to take refuge in the Park Avenue Hotel around the corner. For the brief but hurried trip, the baby's things were packed in her small tin bathtub.

LXXXV

[February ? 1884]

The Organ is moaning – the Bells are bowing, I ask Vinnie what time it is, and she says it is Sunday, so I tell my Pencil to make no noise, and we will go to the House of a Friend "Weeks off," as Dombey said.

Your reunion with Vinnie was amusing and affecting too, and Vinnie still rehearses it to admiring throngs of which Stephen and I are the thrilled components. I think Vinnie has grown since the interview, certainly intellectually, which is the only Bone whose Expanse we woo.

Your flight from the "Sewer" reminded me of the "Mill on the Floss," though "Maggie Tulliver" was missing, and had she been there, her Destiny could not have been packed in the "Bath Tub," though Baby's may be as darkly sweet in the Future running to meet her.

How quickly a House can be deserted, and your infinite inference that the "Soul's poor Cottage" may lose it's Tenant so, was vaster than you thought, and still overtakes me.

How few suggestions germinate!

I shall make Wine Jelly Tonight and send you a Tumbler in the Letter, if the Letter consents, a Fabric sometimes obdurate.

It is warm you are better, and was very cold all the while you were ill.

Baby's flight will embellish History with Gilpin's and Revere's.

With love untold,

Your Emily.

After receiving the last letter, Mrs. Holland may have written her own account of her meeting with Lavinia, asking "Did Vinnie tell you . . .?" for Emily's answer gave some of the details as she vividly saw them after hearing Lavinia's colorful narrative. It is disappointing that Emily's picture does not provide us with enough clues to make the incident clear, so that we could share her amusement over an apparently awkward situation which Lavinia's dramatic sense turned into an adventure.

Emily added this picture as a postscript to a letter whose tone was one of loneliness – for she had lost another friend. Judge Lord of Salem died the thirteenth of March 1884. He was well known throughout the state, and the *Springfield Republican* carried an obituary article the next day, describing him as follows:

> He was an able and upright judge, with strong characteristics that hardened into something like crotchets in his later years. . . In private life Judge Lord was a most interesting man, full of brilliant conversation and kindly impulses and domestic habits.

While his public manner was one of rigorous duty, something more tender that lay behind it was touched by the special quality of Emily's mind, and throughout her life there had been a warm attachment between them.

LXXXVI

[March 1884]

When I tell my sweet Mrs Holland that I have lost another friend, she will not wonder I do not write, but that I raise my Heart to a drooping syllable. Dear Mr Lord has left us. After a brief unconsciousness, a Sleep that ended with a smile, so his Nieces tell us, he hastened away, "seen," we trust, "of Angels" – "Who knows that secret deep" – "Alas, not I."

Forgive the Tears that fell for few, but that few too many, for was not each a World?

Your last dear words seemed stronger, and smiling in the feeling that you were to be, this latest sorrow came. I hope your own are with you, and may not be taken. I hope there is no Dart advancing or in store.

Quite empty, quite at rest,
The Robin locks her Nest, and tries her Wings.
She does not know a Route
But puts her Craft about
For *rumored* Springs.
She does not ask for Noon –
She does not ask for Boon,
Crumbless and homeless, of but one request –
The Birds she lost.

Do you remember writing to us you should "write with the Robins?" They are writing *now*, their Desk in every passing Tree, but the Magic of Mates that cannot hear them, makes their Letters dim.

Later –

Vinnie described it all – The going up to take Medicine and forgetting to return – How many times I have taken that very Medicine myself, with lasting benefit! The Jelly and the pink Cheek, the little clutchings at her frame, to make the grace secure, that had too many Wings. Vinnie omitted nothing, and I followed her around, never hearing enough of that mysterious interview, for was it not a lisp from the irrevocable?

Within that little Hive
Such Hints of Honey lay
As made Reality a Dream
And Dreams, Reality.

Emily

In New England frost may come at any time, and though infrequent as late as Memorial Day, it is not surprising to learn from records kept in Amherst that the temperature dropped to freezing point on the nights of May twenty-ninth, thirtieth, and thirty-first, 1884. Mrs. Holland had already gone to Bonniecastle for the summer, where the weather might be expected to be equally cold. In writing of her move she gave an account of an exploit of Ted's as he was about to complete his law course at Columbia University. At that time the school had two prize fellows whose duties included giving the students oral quizzes in the evenings. It was probably while being subjected to one of these tests that Ted gave his argumentative powers free play, and succeeded in silencing his opponents.

Since Emily's illness in the previous autumn, following the tragic loss of her little nephew Gilbert, she had not mentioned in her letters the child whose death left such a wide gap in her life. Perhaps she found it impossible to speak of a grief she had not been able to assimilate, but now the simple act of sending flowers to decorate his grave on Memorial Day may have helped to turn the loss into an accepted fact and made expression possible.

LXXXVII

[1 June 1884]

Sweet friend.

I hope you brought your open Fire with you, else your confiding Nose has ere this been nipped.

Three dazzling Winter Nights have wrecked the budding

Gardens, and the Bobolinks stand as still in the Meadow as if they had never danced.

I hope your Heart has kept you warm – Should I say your Hearts, for you are yet a Banker.

Death cannot plunder half so fast as Fervor can re-earn.

We had one more, "Memorial Day," to whom to carry Blossoms.

Gilbert had Lilies of the Valley, and Father and Mother, Damson-Hawthorn.

When it shall come my turn, I want a Buttercup. Doubtless the Grass will give me one, for does she not revere the Whims of her flitting Children?

I was with you in all the loneliness, when you took your flight, for every jostling of the Spirit barbs the Loss afresh – even the coming out of the Sun after an Hour's Rain, intensifies their Absence.

Ask some kind Voice to read to you Mark Antony's Oration over his Playmate Caesar.

I never knew a broken Heart to break itself so sweet.

I am glad if Theodore balked the Professors. Most such are Manikins, and a warm blow from a brave Anatomy, hurls them into Wherefores.

A few days later Emily was taken acutely ill. At the end of July she wrote to the Misses Norcross, "Eight Saturday noons ago, I was making a loaf of cake with Maggie, when I saw a great darkness coming and knew no more until late at night. . . The doctor calls it 'revenge of the nerves,' but who but Death had wronged them?" (*Letters*, pp. 268–269). This sudden illness can be exactly dated, for in the same letter to her cousins, who now lived in Concord, Emily referred to a lecture given there by F. B. Sanborn, an account of which she had read that morning in the *Springfield Republican.* The lecture was given before the Concord School of Philosophy on Monday, July twenty-eighth, and was reported in the next day's paper. The eighth Saturday before the twenty-ninth of July was the seventh of June.

In spite of her slow recovery, Emily seems to have written the next two letters during that summer, after the acute phase of her illness was past. The first letter was addressed to Theodore in answer to one he had written her, apparently accompanied by a picture of his own making. It is unfortunate that when this letter was shown to him more than forty years later he had forgotten the subject of it, and although in later life outdoor sketching became his hobby, he could not recall that he had ever painted at that time. However, we can suggest an appropriate occasion for a sketch by imagining that when Ted joined his mother at Bonniecastle and read in Emily's last letter her version of his recent battle with the "professors," he was moved to produce for her amusement during her illness an illustration of those august persons being "hurled into wherefores." Ted's quick wit, inherited from his mother and transmuted into a subtly colored humor of his own, came often into play, and the mock formality of his style, which Emily mimicked in her reply, is more than likely to have been calculated to bring from her just such a response as she gave him.

LXXXVIII

[To Theodore Holland]

[Summer ? 1884]

Dear Sir.

Your request to "remain sincerely" mine demands investigation, and if after synopsis of your career all should seem correct, I am tersely your's.

I shall try to wear the unmerited honor with becoming volume.

Commend me to your Kindred, for whom although a Stranger, I entertain esteem.

I approve the Paint – a study of the Soudan, I take it, but the Scripture assures us our Hearts are all Dongola.

E. Dickinson.

"Cousin Vinnie's" smile.

The second letter written that summer is entirely unrelated to those that precede and those that follow, and nothing in its content betrays its date. It has been placed here because the paper and handwriting fit with those in the sequence, while its reference to garden pests shows that it was written in summer.

Even in her own days of weakness Emily's solicitude for anyone who was suffering remained actively alive. She seems to have written a letter which has not been preserved, asking Mrs. Holland's advice on behalf of an overburdened seamstress whose welfare had long been the concern of her family. The woman, whose name has not been identified, was now having trouble with her eyes. Mrs. Holland had answered at once, giving the name of her New York oculist, Dr. Agnew. Emily had delayed her thanks, hoping to have a report to send from the seamstress, but hearing nothing she decided to wait no longer.

LXXXIX

[Summer 1884]

The immediate and accurate loveliness deserved an immediate reply, but I have been hoping all the Days to hear from my poor friend, who I fear has taken fright anew, and gone to Dr Agnew. She has been much in our family, assisting in many crises, and was it not crisis all the time, in our hurrying Home? The support of a Mother, an almost imbecile

Husband and two very sweet little Girls, hangs upon her Needle, so her sight is not luxury, but necessity.

Father valued her much, often befriending her, and I love to fulfill the kindness only Death suspends.

Forgive the personality. It seemed inevitable, and thank you again for the full sweetness, to which as to a Reservoir the smaller Waters go. What a beautiful Word "Waters" is! When I slept in the Pond and ate Seraphs for Breakfast, I thought I should know all about it now, but "Now" comes, and I dont.

I hear you are feasting on Army Worms, Canker Worms, and Cut Worms, and envy you your Salad.

We had a gallant Rain last Night, the first for many Days, and the Road is full of little Mirrors, at which the Grass adorns itself, when Nobody is seeing – reminding me of an instance similar, "Turn thou mine Eyes away from beholding Vanity!" Love of us each.

Emily.

In September 1884, Kate and Bleecker Van Wagenen visited the Seelyes in Northampton, and Mrs. Seelye's diary for September seventeenth shows the entry: "Kate and Mr. Van W. drove to Amherst and Ashfield." On this visit they inaugurated a custom which they kept up for many years – to leave their family for a week in the autumn and go on a driving trip. Later, when they owned their own horses, the tour started from home in the family "trap," but on this occasion they made Northampton the point of departure for trips by the day, and the local livery stable probably provided the outfit. As the round trip could not be much less than forty miles, the call at Amherst must have been very brief. They were welcomed by Lavinia, who was, according to Emily, not only pleased with "the Gentleman with the vast Name" as a person, but impressed with his position as a member of the publishing firm of Dodd, Mead and Company. They did not meet Emily.

At about this time Emily wrote to Colonel Higginson that she had spent her summer in a chair, but was "again abroad" (*Letters,* p. 319). In spite of this improvement in her health, it seems to have been fully understood that she would not have been expected to receive the visitors herself.

XC

[Late September 1884]

Dear Sister.

To have been in the actual presence of "Dodd, Mead, and Co" is impressive to Vinnie, and she says every day, "I thought we should hear from Mrs-Holland," she being the Chairman of that loved Assembly. Vinnie was charmed with the Stranger. With Kate, she had been always charmed, so the spell was complete. But she found him a dark Man – the Picture depicted him a light. That, she requires explained. Vinnie much regretted that she was'nt in Court Costume, but I told her that high topped Boots would'nt have been expected, which was not the comfort that I could wish.

Autumn is among us, though almost unperceived – and the Cricket sings in the morning, now, a most pathetic conduct.

We have no Fruit this year, the Frost having barreled that in the Bud – except the "Fruits of the Spirit," but Vinnie prefers Baldwins.

Thank Kate and the Consort, for their beloved visages – the "surprise parties" of Saints are ineffable, and when they bring the assurance of the loved convalescence, they are even more beatific –

Emily.

While the Van Wagenens were making their autumn tour, Mrs. Holland kept her little granddaughter with her at Bonniecastle, taking her back to New York to rejoin her parents when they returned. With the leaves flying and Election Day not far off, the end of October is approaching when Emily writes again. The anniversary of which she speaks was doubtless that of Dr. Holland's death on the twelfth of October.

XCI

[Late October 1884]

Dear One.

Upon the presumption that the "Swallows homeward" flew, I address to their Nest, as formerly. I trust "the Airs were delicate" the Day they made their flight, and that they still sing Life's portentous Music. I feared you would steal the Grandchild in the Parents' absence, but then it would be such a happy theft, so joyful to the robbed, and to the Thief presiding. Could Jurisprudence sigh? I hope the Lass is hearty, loving and beloved. I know she is Grandmama's Tonic – but which is the biggest, the Patient or the Medicine? You always were a Wren, you know, the tenant of a Twig.

The Leaves are flying high away, and the Heart flies with them, though where that wondrous Firm alight, is not "an open secret." What a curious Lie that phrase is! I see it of Politicians. Before I write to you again, we shall have had a new Czar. Is the Sister a Patriot?

"George Washington was the Father of his Country" – "George Who?"

That sums all Politics to me – but then I love the Drums, and they are busy now.

I did not forget the Anniversary you so tenderly marked,

but cover it with Leaves, as it was long since covered with Honor – which is better than Leaves. To put one's Hand on the sacred figures, is like touching "the Ark of the Covenant."

All grows strangely emphatic, and I think if I should see you again, I sh'd begin every sentence with "I say unto you." The Bible dealt with the Centre, not with the Circumference.

Emily,

With love.

It is doubtful whether Mrs. Holland ever saw Emily during the years that remained to her after Gilbert's death, and only a few letters are left to complete the record of the friendship. The next letter, written early in February 1885, implies that Mrs. Holland had visited in Northampton without going to Amherst, and that Lavinia had gone to see her there. The value Lavinia set on Mrs. Holland's appreciation of her on that occasion, when she was apart from her sister, suggests that when the two were together Lavinia's deep and admiring devotion to Emily often caused her to accept a secondary place. Some time must have passed since their meeting, when Mrs. Holland, who had a tendency to rheumatism, had spoken of her dread of the winter's cold. By February her foreboding was justified by an attack that brought from Emily a vehement denunciation of the disease that caused her friend to suffer.

XCII

[February 1885]

Dear Sister,

Horace, the wise, but acrid Man who so long lived with us, was pleased to say of what displeased him, "I hate it, I despise it," and I feel an animadversion similar to the Rheumatism. To wring your bonnie shoulder, how brutal, how malign!

Were Revenge accessible, I would surely wreak it, but that, like all the rest of us, is an Apparition.

I trust he will discontinue you for something more befitting. I shall then seek the "Letter" which the "Weird Woman promised" me.

The Winter which you feared has shrunk to February, which limited Expanse has the enchantment of the last, and is therefore beloved. "But the last Leaf fear to touch," says the consummate Browning.

Tell Katrina about the Buttercups that Emily tills, and the Butterflies Emily chases, not catches, alas, because her Hat is torn – but not half so ragged as her Heart, which is barefoot always.

Vinnie wrote you a few Days since, and is sure if you value her as much as you did in Northampton, you will soon reply!

Love for all but the Rheumatism –

Always,

Emily.

On the ninth of February Mrs. Holland's second grandchild was born: a boy, to whom his parents gave a name even vaster than his father's – Garrat Bleecker Van Wagenen. Emily never mentioned him by name, but she did send congratulations, not altogether unqualified, to his mother, several weeks later. By that time she had read the March number of *The Century*, which came out late in February, and its contents had become sufficiently mingled in her mind with those of other issues as to leave her uncertain in which number she had seen a picture that particularly amused her. It was the March number, however, that contained the engraving to which she referred. Used as a frontispiece, it was an illustration for an article of reminiscences of Daniel Webster by Stephen M. Allen, and was taken from a daguerreotype of the statesman wearing a beaver hat of heroic size, which must have made an absurd contrast to the low-crowned "derbies" of the 1880's.

XCIII

[Early March 1885]

So Madonna and Daughter were incomplete, and Madonna and Son, must supersede!

Perhaps the Picture is right. But is'nt it rather cool Weather for the Wise Men of the East?

Perhaps their Shining Overcoats obviate the Climate.

The young Man is doubtless an acquisition, but I uphold Katrina, and any encroachment upon her, shall resent to the last.

Congratulate the New Moon on her second Star, and with love for each, and a "Dont wake the Baby," we are heartfeltly

Emily.

Rejoice that you are better.

One more word for Baby –

I send him *Daniel Webster's Hat* for his Golden Wedding. It can be found in the "Century" –

March Number, I think.

Be sure and try it on –

While little Garrat was still young enough to be the new element in his grandmother's life, Emily wrote the following letter which continues the "Holy Family" theme begun in the last one with the figure of "Madonna and Son." Written only a little more than a year before she died, this letter contains one of the most remarkable passages in the whole series, and it is very disappointing not to be able to throw a clear light on the story that lies behind it.

The letter is an answer to one Mrs. Holland had written with her own hand, telling about a controversy in the press or the talk of the day over the character of a prominent woman in whom she and Emily were both interested. Emily's reply, full of respect for the freedom of another's individuality, points out that such contention only enhances the person's importance. The papers of the time give no hint of a social scandal that would have had meaning for the two women, nor has anything been found to fit the case in the lives of their personal friends. One is inclined to look for the answer in an entirely different field.

Emily had been waiting eagerly for the publication of the *Life of George Eliot* by her husband, J. W. Cross (*Letters*, p. 318), which was brought out early in February, 1885. It was one of the important books of the year and received much attention in newspapers and periodicals during February, March, and April. Perhaps Mrs. Holland, knowing how interested Emily would be, had collected as many of these criticisms as she could and sent them to her. Most of the writers greeted the book with enthusiam, though some found it disappointing that it did not make more revelations regarding George Eliot's life and character. Only the highest admiration for her gifts and her personal character was expressed in most instances. *The Critic* for the seventh of February said, "To read it is a liberal education . . . not the broadening of one's nature in any definite direction, but the lifting of one's whole nature to a higher level. . ." On the other hand, the New York *Observer*, representing the conventional Christian attitude, dwelt chiefly on her unbelief and sin, and wondered how she was able to write so much "with such a load on her soul." Here is plenty of material for controversy, which would have been of vital interest to such a devoted reader of George Eliot's books as Emily had been.

XCIV

[Spring 1885]

Dear Sister,

To "gain the whole World" in the Evening Mail, without the baleful forfeit hinted in the Scripture, was indeed achievement – and I was led resisting to Bed, but Vinnie was firm as the Soudan.

Thank you tenderly. I was breathlessly interested.

Contention "loves a shining Mark." Only *fight* about me, said the dying King, and my Crown is sure.

It is only the Moss upon my Throne that impairs my Dying.

None of us know her enough to judge her, so her Maker must be her "Crowner's Quest" – Saul criticized his Savior till he became enamored of him – then he was less loquacious.

It was lovely to see your Hand again in the old attitude – a literary one, and the Present flew like a Butterfly, and the Past *was*, but there we must not linger – too many linger with us.

Love for the "Holy Family," and say to the Son that the Little Boy in the Trinity had no Grandmama, only a Holy Ghost.

But you must go to Sleep. I, who sleep always, need no Bed.

Foxes have Tenements, and remember, the Speaker was a Carpenter.

Emily.

Emily was again taken ill in the autumn of 1885, and spent the whole winter in her room. She wrote to the Misses Norcross in March that she had passed through two long periods of illness, with a short respite between (*Letters*, p. 427), and probably about the same time she told Colonel Higginson, in a letter to which no date has been given, that she had been "bereft of book or thought by the doctor's reproof" (*Letters*, p. 321). After Christmas she had been too ill to thank Mrs. Holland for her gift. By early spring she had improved enough to resume writing, and reached out eagerly once more toward those whose affection meant much to her. The following letter, almost pathetic in the restraint with which she asks for news, lest her demand be a burden, is, so far as we know, the last she wrote to this old friend with whom she had kept a close connection for more than thirty years.

Mrs. Holland, meanwhile, had gone south to spend several months in St. Augustine, Florida, in order to escape the attacks of rheumatism she had experienced in recent winters in New York. She took one of her nieces, a daughter of her sister Amelia, with her as a companion, and the experiment was so successful that she continued to make the trip every winter until the end of her life in 1896. It is hard to tell whether the flowers for which Emily sends thanks had actually taken the long journey from Florida, or whether they were the product of a northern hothouse, sent as a parting gift before Mrs. Holland started her journey.

XCV

[March? 1886]

Concerning the little sister, not to assault, not to adjure, but to obtain those constancies which exalt friends, we followed her to St. Augustine, since which the trail was lost, or says George Stearns of his alligator, "there was no such aspect."

The beautiful blossoms waned at last, the charm of all who knew them, resisting the effort of earth or air to persuade them to root, as the great florist says, "The flower that never will in other climate grow."

To thank you for its fragrance would be impossible, but then its other blissful traits are more than can be numbered. And the beloved Christmas, too, for which I never thanked you. I hope the little heart is well, – *big* would have been the width, – and the health solaced; any news of her as sweet as the first arbutus.

Emily and Vinnie give the love greater every hour.

With "love greater every hour" the letters come to an end. We must assume that Emily's appeal brought a prompt answer from Mrs.

Holland, whose affection never faltered, though her writing sometimes failed. It is doubtful whether she had any intimation that her friend would not recover. Sickness to Emily was a private affair, and she was not interested in symptoms or the names of diseases. Lavinia carried the weight of material responsibility for her and devotedly protected her to the end. Spring lent fresh strength, and during the last month or two she was not wholly an invalid. She did not know until a few days before death came that she, who had passed through its mystery vicariously so many times, was soon to experience it herself. On the fifteenth of May 1886, in the full glory of spring, she slipped quietly through the narrow door between mortal and immortal that for her had long stood half open.

The only news I know
Is bulletins all day
From Immortality.

The only shows I see
To-morrow and To-day,
Perchance Eternity.

The only One I meet
Is God, — the only street
Existence, this traversed

If other news there be,
Or admirabler show —
I'll tell it you.

NOTES

LETTER I

Emily's quotations from the Bible are often inexact, and in many instances she paraphrased the passages. The references given in these notes are to the original sources, so far as I have been able to trace them, and are given without comment on the changes she made in using them.

don't find. "I seek and I don't find," Matthew 7:7,8, also Luke 11:9,10.

scorpion. "when they ask an egg, they get a scorpion," Luke 12:12.

Adolphus Hawkins, Esq. A character in Longfellow's prose romance, *Kavanagh.* In him the author satirizes the village poets whose effusions filled the small town journals of the period.

immortality. "'this mortal' essays immortality," I Corinthians 15:53.

Moral Law. To discipline herself out of the Hawkins mood, Emily thought of Dr. Heman Humphrey, president of Amherst College from 1823 to 1845, who must have been an august figure among his fellow townsmen in Emily's childhood. He taught mental and moral philosophy, and was a national leader in the temperance movement.

read it eagerly. Among the "funny accidents" in the *Springfield Republican* of the time I have found no reports of "gentlemen in factories" getting "their heads cut off quite informally," but the writer of the column in which such reports appeared seems to have been impressed by their frequency, for on the first of October 1853, he wrote,

> On looking over our summary for the week we find that we have chronicled ten deaths from railroad accidents, three by being caught in machinery, three from burns and scalds, four from the falling of buildings, seven from falls, and seven by drowning.

A good example of "where railroads meet each other unexpectedly" is shown in the following item in the issue for 22 November 1853:

> Two engines, with their accompanying baggage cars and six passenger cars were pretty effectually used up by a collision on the Baltimore and Susquehanna Railroad on Friday morning. The only persons injured were the conductors, and their injuries were trifling. It gives us great pleasure to add, as a novelty, that nobody was to blame.

If Emily read the paper the previous winter she would certainly have enjoyed the following, from the *Republican* of 19 January 1852:

> A train from New York for Philadelphia Friday, when passing Bristol, ran into a car house, and driving out an empty car, sent it through the dining room of an adjoining house. Mr. Stewart, the owner of the house, and his family, were at dinner, and were buried in the ruins, but their injuries were not serious. James Kinley and James Lexor, firemen, had each a foot crushed, and amputation was found necessary in both cases. No passengers were hurt.

LETTER III

crimson children. The figure of "the crimson children" is also found in a letter which Madame Bianchi states was written to Susan Gilbert at Baltimore in the late winter of 1855 (*Emily Dickinson Face to Face,* p. 212). Since it has now been proved that Susan Gilbert was in Baltimore in 1852, the heading must be incorrect, for Emily mentions the Reverend and Mrs. Dwight, who did not come to Amherst until August 1853. The letter may prove to have been written at about the same time as the one to the Hollands.

will return. The stanza of poetry which forms the last paragraph of this letter is given here as prose, just as it was first printed. It appears also as part of a poem in *Emily Dickinson Face to Face,* p. 181, dated 1848 by Madame Bianchi, who stated that it was probably the earliest poem Emily sent to Susan Gilbert.

Emily. Emily's usual spelling of her name at this time was "Emilie," but another example of the use of "Emily" is found in a letter to her brother probably written a short time before this (*Letters*, p. 116).

LETTER VI

Mary Powell. The Maiden and Married Life of Mary Powell is the title of a book by Ann Manning, published in 1852, which the publishers' advertisement describes as a "nicely drawn and more poetical version" of the story of John Milton's first wife. Emily may be suggesting that the book itself, which she and the Hollands might have discussed at the time of her recent visit, be abandoned when they moved; or it is possible that she is referring to some situation the Hollands had observed in a neighbor's family similar to that described in the book.

LETTER VII

the cherry-tree. "Pray, Mr. Whately, what is *that* upon the cherry tree?" Whately's *Logic* and *Rhetoric*, published in London in 1826 and 1828 respectively, reached many editions, and seem to have been used in the American schools.

not made with hands. "We shall sit in a parlor 'not made with hands.'" II Corinthians 5:1.

exquisite hymn. Dr. Holland's "exquisite hymn," for which Emily sent thanks may have been his Christmas carol, beginning "There's a song in the air," which was probably written at about this time. It was not published in the *Springfield Republican* during the Christmas season of 1855, however, and if it was the poem to which Emily referred, she probably read a manuscript copy enclosed in Mrs. Holland's letter. Since Emily's use of the word "hymn" was not confined to religious poems, it is also possible that she was referring to some verses of less lasting merit that were published in the *Springfield Republican* on the first of January under the title "Things New and Old" and which were signed with his initials. With a sweeping disregard of the past, natural, perhaps, to a young man who has to make his own way in the world, he says

Better the morning's silver dew
Than the evening's river of gold –
Better a thousand fold!

On the twelfth of January the *Republican* printed a contribution from a reader, Mrs. F. H. Cooke, written in the same meter as Dr. Holland's, expressing her vehement disagreement with his sentiments in verses bearing the title "The Old and the New," which begin with down-to-earth realism,

The new is a springtime brown
When the bluebird shudders with cold.

Possibly Emily had read both, and her thanks may be a tactful expression of her loyalty to her friend.

LETTER VIII

In 1862 Emily wrote to Thomas Wentworth Higginson:

> You inquire my books. For poets, I have Keats, and Mr. and Mrs. Browning. For prose, Mr. Ruskin, Sir Thomas Browne, and the *Revelations*.
>
> (*Letters*, p. 273).

go no more out. Revelation 3:12.

no tears. Revelation 21:4.

four thousand. "the hundred and forty and four thousand," Revelation 14:3.

up to Heaven. "'parted' as we walked, and 'snatched up to Heaven,'" Luke 24:51.

name is Death. "There is a Reaper, whose name is Death," is the opening line of Longfellow's poem, "The Reaper and the Flowers." It was included in his first volume of poems, *Voices of the Night,* published in 1839.

LETTER IX

it was said. "Lips which sealed as soon as it was said" probably refers to Ben Newton, who died the twenty-fourth of March 1853. It was of him she wrote to Colonel Higginson: "I had a friend who taught me Immortality; but venturing too near, himself, he never returned."

Remember me today. The thief's request—"Remember me today," is from Luke 23: 42, 43.

the Lamb's Book. The concept of the Book of Life is found in both the Old and New Testaments, but the "Lamb's Book" is a phrase used only in Revelation. 21:27.

LETTER X

Mr. Chapman. I am indebted to Rebecca Patterson for information regarding the date and purpose of the visit to Amherst of Judge Chapman and Mr. Hyde.

evening with ——. Susan Gilbert Dickinson's name was consistently deleted from the text of *Letters of Emily Dickinson* at her own request, but there is no difficulty in identifying the person alluded to in this and other letters (See XVIII). Mrs. Todd's transcript of this letter from the original, kindly loaned me by her daughter, Millicent Todd Bingham, shows an "S" followed by a dash to indicate the name.

in Newgate. The name of Newgate Prison in London is almost as familiar a byword in English literature as "Bedlam." Emily would have found it, not only in her contemporary Dickens, but as far back as Shakespeare, where it appears in *Henry the Fourth,* Act III, Scene 3.

Falstaff: How now, lad? is the wind in that door, i' faith? must we all march?
Bardolph: Yes, two and two, Newgate-fashion.

LETTER XI

Cockneys. Emily's association of cardinals and cockneys is so startling that one wonders what brought each of them to her attention. It is gratifying to find a probable source for her opinion of the character of cardinals in a play which she must have seen discussed in the press during the years just preceding the one in which this letter was written. Bulwer-Lytton's *Richelieu,* first produced in 1839, had become very popular on the American stage, and between 1857 and 1859 both Edwin Booth and Barry Sullivan had been seen in the leading role. Possibly Emily's brother Austin had seen the play and given her a first hand report of it. There does not seem to be any immediate cause for her interest in cockneys, but her reading would have given her plenty of opportunity to become acquainted with them. Aside from those she met in the novels of Dickens, she must have seen them often referred to by other writers. She probably read Emerson's *English Traits* when it was published in 1856, and found in it the expression "cockney conceit," which occurs in the second chapter, as well as the considerable emphasis on the national pride of the British in a later chapter. Her father's library probably contained Hazlitt's essays, among them his *Table Talk,* in which the chapter "On Londoners and Country People" speaks of the attitude of superiority to be found in the true cockney.

LETTER XII

whole legions. For "whole legions" of daisies, see note on "Whole legions of angels" (Letter XVI).

The gentian. The gentian is the first flower of autumn in the New England meadows. Emily is using it as an indication of the approach of death.

LETTER XVI

Since the manuscripts of this letter and the poem at the end of Part One are the only examples of Emily's handwriting between 1853 and 1862 to which I have had access, the letter was dated by internal evidence only. According to information which was not available until after the book was in proof, the writing shows characteristics which place it in 1857 or 1858. It may prove to have been written in March 1858, the first year in which Dr. Holland made a prolonged lecture tour.

of Sheffield. In "Mr. Brown of Sheffield" Emily either inadvertently or purposely used another name in making use of a sobriquet taken from a passage in Dickens' *David Copperfield,* in which "Brooks of Sheffield" is used to designate a person who should remain nameless. This passage is found in Chapter 2, in a conversation carried on between Mr. Murdstone and his friends over the head of the curious little David. Emily used the pseudonym again many years later, in Letter LXXX, giving it that time correctly.

legions of angels. The phrase "whole legions of Angels" may have been suggested by Matthew 26:53; "Thinkest thou that I can not now pray to my father, and he shall presently give me more than twelve legions of angels?" But Emily was also familiar with Milton's *Paradise Lost,* in which the armies of angels are spoken of as legions throughout the poem. The phrase "whole legions" occurs in Book 6, line 655:

> Themselves invaded next, and on their heads
> Main promontories flung, which in the air
> Came shadowing, and oppressed whole legions armed.

LETTER XIX

treasure is. "Where the treasure is," Matthew 6:21, Luke 12:34.

LETTER XX

sea or land. "The light that never was on sea or land" is found in the fourth stanza of Wordsworth's *Elegiac Stanzas, Suggested by a Picture of Peele Castle in a Storm, by Sir George Beaumont.*

LETTER XXIII

Dr. Vaill. Although this letter was first published under the date 1877, the reference to Dr. Vaill fixes the time before 1868. The Reverend Joseph Vaill was a prominent Congregational minister who was pastor of a church in Palmer from 1854 to 1867. In addition to more than thirty years of parish work, he had done a valuable service to Amherst College as general agent at a time when the college was in financial straits. He spent the last year of his life as a member of the Massachusetts General Court, and died in 1869. The last year in which the letter could have been written was 1867, but the exact date cannot be fixed because the existing records of Dr. Vaill's church do not show that Dr. Holland ever preached there.

LETTER XXVI

Mob at last. Emily's favorite meeting place, the "Northwest Passage," is described by Martha Dickinson Bianchi in *Emily Dickinson Face to Face,* p. 25.

Darwin does not tell us. Darwin's *The Descent of Man* was published in 1871, the year when this letter was written. *The Origin of Species* was published in 1859, and *Variation of Animals and Plants under Domestication* in 1868. It does not seem probable that Emily would have seen the first edition of *The Various Contrivances by which Orchids are Fertilized by Insects,* published in London in 1862. The revised American edition did not appear until 1877.

LETTER XXVII

he punisheth. "whom he loveth, he punisheth," Hebrews 12:6.

the Gingerbread triumphed. Emily Dickinson's recipe for gingerbread, which this letter implies she had sent to Mrs. Holland, is given in *Emily Dickinson Face to Face,* p. 230.

LETTER XXIX

in thy Sight. "Even so, Father, for so it seemed faithful [good] in thy Sight." Matthew 11:26.

LETTER XXX

put on Incorruption. ". . . this Corruptible shall put on Incorruption." I Corinthians 15:42.

LETTER XXXI

have chosen. "I have chosen whom I have chosen." John 13:18.

another World. Emily's remarks on the conflict between science and the Bible reflect the widespread disturbance of mind that led to much discussion of the subject in the press of the day. Just at this time Dr. Holland published a series of articles on "Modern scepticism" by the Reverend Augustus Blauvelt, whose writings had much to do with the introduction to the American public of the higher criticism of the Bible. The articles appeared in *Scribner's Monthly* for August, September, and October, 1873. A second series was published the following year, attempting to reconcile scientific and religious thought in regard to supernaturalism, miracles, and the resurrection of Christ.

LETTER XXXII

one Pearl. "Every several Gate was of one Pearl." Revelation 21:21.

LETTER XXXIII

the Right. "the 'Left Hand' circumvent the Right!" Matthew 6:3,4.

the Chamber-Window. On the thirteenth of May 1874 the *Amherst Record* announced that Maginley's Circus would appear on the twenty-third, and present "The most stupendous free street tournament" ever given by American capital. In the procession would be "The great Golden Appolonican drawn by forty horses, and the largest elephant in the world."

LETTER XXXIV

unto the Dust. "Dust unto the Dust," familiar words used in the burial service, probably have their source in Ecclesiastes 3:20 ("All go into one place; all are of the dust, and all turn to dust again"). Emily was probably referring to the words as found in the burial service, however, where the "final clause" is: "looking for the general Resurrection in the last day, and the life of the world to come, through our Lord Jesus Christ."

rejoins Argemone. Charles Kingsley was one of the novelists whose work Emily knew well, and his death, the twenty-third of January 1875, could not pass unnoticed. Argemone is the name of the heroine of his first novel, *Yeast*, who died of a fever contracted while visiting the homes of her father's tenants, whose condition filled her with remorse.

LETTER XXXV

render his friend. "the Psalmist who knew not what to render his friend," Psalms 116:12.

LETTER XXXVI

no Burden, Jane. "I find your benefits no burden, Jane," is from Charlotte Brontë's *Jane Eyre,* Chapter 15, in which Rochester thanks Jane for saving his life when his demented wife had set fire to his bed curtains. He preferred to accept nothing from others, but *Jane's* "benefits" were no burden to him.

LETTER XXXVIII

of the Regiment. In "The Child of the Regiment" Emily may have been thinking of the chapter called "The Baby of the Regiment" in Thomas Wentworth Higginson's book *Army Life in a Black Regiment,* published in 1870.

accept us all. The connection of Dr. Holland's "growing fame" with Stratford on Avon is not clear, but as Emily's allusions can usually be found to have some specific meaning, it is worth while to consider the possibility of his having been invited to attend the ceremonies at the laying of the cornerstone of the Shakespeare Memorial Theatre at Stratford on the twenty-third of April 1877. A friend of his, Miss Kate Field, an American actress and author who was a contributor to *Scribner's Monthly,* was living at Stratford at the time, and when the theater was opened two years later she took part in the program.

LETTER XL

tender and true. Dinah Maria Craik (Miss Mulock) wrote the poem *Douglas, Douglas, tender and true,* which was set to music and included in the popular song books of the time. It was derived from an early ballad.

come tomorrow. The scene of Little Nell's Grandfather at her grave is from Dickens' *Old Curiosity Shop,* Chapter 72.

ever seen. "Sweetest eyes were ever seen" is from Mrs. Browning's "Catarina to Camoens (dying in his absence abroad, and referring to the poem in which he recorded the sweetness of her eyes)." Another allusion to this poem is made in Letter LXXV.

LETTER XLII

every day. "angry with the Wicked – every Day." Psalms 7:11.

Nicholas Minturn. Dr. Holland's last novel, *Nicholas Minturn,* was appearing serially at this time in *Scribner's Monthly*, running from December 1876 to October 1877. Emily does not tell us what she thought of it herself, but reports on the enthusiasm of the elderly couple, Deacon and Mrs. Luke Sweetser, whose land adjoined the Dickinsons' on the north. They are not to be confused with the Joseph Sweetsers, who were related to the Dickinsons. Mrs. Joseph Sweetser was Mr. Dickinson's sister Catherine.

LETTER XLIII

present so divine. Emily remembers a hymn she used to know, in which the words "A present so divine" might easily have been the child's version of "A presence so divine." But as there appears to be no hymn in the collections she was likely to know containing either of those expressions, it is possible that the sound of the words as heard in the last verse of "When I survey the wondrous Cross" might have slid together in her memory.

> Were the whole realm of nature mine,
> That were a present far too small;
> Love so amazing, so divine
> Demands my soul, my life, my all.

LETTER XLV

forgot the Port. Emily's apt figure of the "blameless ship that forgot the port" has not been found in any of the works of Hawthorne, to whom she attributed it. In recalling something she had read years before, she may have been mistaken about the author.

LETTER XLVI

time has made. "The Soul's poor Cottage" is inaccurately quoted from a poem by Edmund Waller, entitled in early editions of his work

"Of the last verses in the book," but standing under various titles in the anthologies where it is used. The lines are:

> The soul's dark cottage, batter'd and decayed,
> Lets in new light through chinks which time has made.

the Sunbeams play. "About" *which* "ranks the sunbeams play" was probably suggested by "Lines written to a march, in imitation of a military band" by Reginald Heber, Bishop of Calcutta. The opening lines of the poem are:

> I see them on their winding way,
> Above their ranks the moonbeams play.

The identity of those who formed the ranks is never explained, and the reader is never quite sure whether they belong this side of the grave or the other.

abide or no. The last four lines of the poem "These held their Wick above the West" were used in a variant version in a note to Mrs. Austin Dickinson (*Emily Dickinson Face to Face*, p. 265), and written as prose in a letter to T. W. Higginson (*Letters*, p. 302).

LETTER XLVII

little Basket. "Mrs. Browning's little Basket." The "basket" was one of Emily's favorite images. An indispensable article in a country household, it held for her special connotations of fullness or preciousness. She wrote to her cousins in 1868 (*Letters*, p. 236), "Tell us all the load. Amherst's little basket is never so full but it holds more. That's a basket's cause." Whatever carried a precious load, whether it was her heart or a piece of paper, became a basket. So we may assume that this was neither an actual basket of willow or splint nor an allusion to one of Mrs. Browning's poems—for she said "it is not her." The reader's imagination may supply a better explanation than the editor's, whose conjecture is that Emily may have folded the note in a circular notice or the wrapping from a little book recently received in the mail. A small volume of Mrs. Browning's *Earlier Poems* was published for the first time in America the first of March 1878 by

James Miller of New York. The book was reviewed in the *Springfield Republican* on the twelfth of March, and Emily's devotion to Mrs. Browning would have induced her to send for a copy as soon as it was available.

Whips of time. "For who would bear the Whips and Scorns of time," is a line from Hamlet's soliloquy in *Hamlet,* Act III, Scene 1.

LETTER XLVIII

pick arbutus? "Pink, small and punctual," quoted in the editor's comment on this letter, p. 131, is the first line of a poem found in *Poems of Emily Dickinson,* p. 93.

shall be given. "To him that hath, shall be given," Mark 4:25.

LETTER L

Mollie Maguires. The "Mollie Maguires" were a secret organization of Irish miners in Pennsylvania, a branch of the Physical Force Party of Ireland. Between 1854 and 1877 they committed many outrages, including murder, but were finally exposed and the leaders convicted. Nineteen members in all were hanged at four different dates, the twenty-first of June 1877, the twenty-fifth of March 1878, the eighteenth of December 1878, and the fourteenth of January 1879. The last is the date that fits best with other evidence to date this letter, for other examples of the paper on which it was written were used only from October 1879 through 1881. The final hanging was carried out just thirty seconds before a reprieve arrived from the Governor of Pennsylvania, and the *Springfield Republican* of the fifteenth of January gave an important place to the event under the headline "THIRTY SECONDS LATE: Two Mollie Maguires Hanged while a Reprieve Waited at the Door of the Jail." This dramatic and ironic turn of fate was the sort of situation about which Emily's imagination would have played.

his frontier. "The rectification of his Frontier" is probably an allusion to the peace settlements of the Russo-Turkish war of 1877–1878. The Treaty of San Stefano, made the third of March 1878, arranged several adjustments in the boundaries of the Balkan states. Negotiations continued throughout the year, and the treaty between Russia and Turkey was signed on the eighth of February 1879. Notes on the progress of the negotiations continued all through January.

LETTER LI

moral foundations. Mr. Wentworth, with whom Emily identifies herself in her feeling of the instability of her environment, is a character in Henry James' novel, *The Europeans,* published in 1878. He is a conservative Boston gentleman, who, confronted with the possibility of a marriage between his daughter and her cousin from Europe, does not consider her love for him a suitable foundation for their union. "Where are our moral grounds?" demanded Mr. Wentworth, who had always thought Mr. Brand "[another suitor] would be just the thing for a younger daughter with a peculiar temperament" (p. 198). Emily's inexact quotations have been noted before.

Mrs. Pendexter. Mr. Pendexter was the old minister in Longfellow's *Kavanagh,* which Emily had read thirty years before. He was dismissed by his congregation because he spent too much time in farming in order to eke out the scanty living he received as pastor of the church. He and his wife were last seen driving away in their buggy, with a trunk slung underneath, and the old horse shaking the dust of the ungrateful parish defiantly from his hoofs.

LETTER LII

Aunt Glegg. Emily lived with George Eliot's characters as she did with those of Dickens and the Brontës. Aunt Glegg, from *The Mill on the Floss,* was Mrs. Tulliver's sister, who cast a shadow over the family life, whether present or absent. It is probable that Emily was referring to her own Aunt Elizabeth, Mrs. Augustus N. Currier.

Righteousness. "Correction in righteousness," II Timothy 3:16 ("All scripture is given by inspiration of God, and is profitable for doctrine, for reproof, for correction, for instruction in righteousness").

LETTER LIII

a Burden. "the Grasshopper is a Burden." Ecclesiastes 12:5.

LETTER LIV

hight. Emily's use of the spelling *hight* instead of *height* is sanctioned by Webster, and the variation was consistently used in the *Springfield Republican* during her lifetime.

fervent circuit. In "Am not unmindful of the Dew or its fervent circuit" Emily seems to be thinking of the biblical significance of dew as a life-giving blessing from Heaven. There are numerous passages in the Old Testament which she might have had in mind, but one that seems appropriate here is from Isaiah 26:19:

> Thy dead men shall live, together with my dead body shall they arise. Awake and sing, ye that dwell in dust; for thy dew is as the dew of herbs, and the earth shall cast out the dead.

LETTER LV

far better. Philippians 1:23:

> For I am in a strait betwixt two, having a desire to depart, and to be with Christ: which is far better.

more sea. "And there was no more Sea," Revelation 21:1.

Strength be. "As thy Day so shall thy Strength be," Deuteronomy 33:20.

in behalf of Lilies. "Please 'consider' me," Matthew 6:28, Luke 12:27 ("Consider the lilies of the field").

LETTER LVI

lowly Spirit. "a meek and lowly Spirit," Matthew 11:29 ("Take my yoke upon you and learn of me; for I am meek and lowly of heart, and ye shall find rest for your souls").

LETTER LVIII

Mr Samuel. In a letter to Mrs. Samuel Bowles at about this time (*Letters*, p. 213), Emily explains: "Mr. Samuel is his memorial name."

for thee. The sentence beginning "Amazing human heart"—written in prose form, in spite of its poetic quality—was used in a different connection in a letter to the Misses Norcross, dated December, 1880, just after the death of George Eliot (*Letters*, p. 260).

Kingdom of Heaven. "Unless we become as Rogues," Matthew 18:3 ("Except ye be converted, and become as little children, ye shall not enter into the kingdom of heaven").

LETTER LIX

on the tree. "in his own body on the tree," I Peter 2:24:

> Who his own self bare our sins in his own body on the tree, that we, being dead to sins, should live unto righteousness: by whose stripes ye were healed.

LETTER LX

the immortal Peewee. There is a suggestion here of a mischievous smile in the direction of Emily's friend and "tutor" Thomas Wentworth Higginson. In an essay on "The Life of Birds" in the *Atlantic Monthly* for September 1862 – the first year of Emily's correspondence with him, when every word he wrote would have been of interest to her – he said,

> And penetrating to some yet lonelier place, we find it consecrated to that life-long sorrow, whatever it may be, which is made immortal in the plaintive cadence of the Peewee-Flycatcher.

The article was included in a volume of his essays entitled *Outdoor Papers*, published in 1863.

Cap'n Cuttle. Captain Cuttle, a genial old salt, who wore a glazed hat and had a hook in the place of his right hand, was a character in Dickens' *Dombey and Son.* He was full of schemes for the benefit of his friends, and his talk was filled with happy misquotations.

the Doctor promised. The picture of George Eliot which Dr. Holland promised to send, was probably the one used as a frontispiece in the first number of *The Century*, November 1881.

LETTER LXI

Writing Bacon's work. The discussion of the possibility that Shakespeare's plays might have been written by Bacon was started by an American woman, Delia Bacon, whose book, *The Philosophy of the*

Plays of Shakespere Unfolded, was published in 1857. Her theory was that the plays were produced by a literary coterie consisting of Bacon, Raleigh, and Spenser.

LETTER LXII

choice in the Foe. The story of the capture of the Ark of the Covenant by the Philistines is found in I Samuel 4.

LETTER LXIII

Inasmuch. "Inasmuch" refers to the passage in Matthew 25 telling of those who shall inherit the Kingdom, ending: "Inasmuch as ye have done it unto one of the least of these my brethren, ye have done it unto me."

shall lead them. "A little child shall lead them." Isaiah 11:6.

LETTER LXIX

had no mercy. The quotation from Charlotte Brontë about the character of her sister Emily at the time of her illness and death is taken from Mrs. Gaskell's *Life of Charlotte Brontë*, Chapter 2.

we clasp. " 'Whom seeing not, we' clasp" is a paraphrase of I Peter 1:8:

> Whom not having seen, ye love; in whom, though now ye see him not, yet believing ye rejoice with joy unspeakable and full of glory.

LETTER LXXIV

the Holy Ghost. "Holy men, moved by the Holy Ghost," II Peter 1:21. Although Emily probably did ask such a question about the Bible when she was a child, the words of question and answer as given here are reminiscent of those in the catechisms used in the teaching of religion.

LETTER LXXV

What sequel? The two quotations, which Emily states are from the same poem, "*Can* trouble dwell with April days?" and "Of Love that never found its earthly close, what sequel?" are by Tennyson, but are from different poems. The first is from *In Memoriam A. H. H.* (No. 83 in Cambridge Edition):

> Dip down upon the northern shore,
> Oh sweet new-year delaying long;
> Thou doest expectant nature wrong;
> Delaying long, delay no more.
>
> What stays thee from the clouded moons,
> Thy sweetness from its proper place?
> Can trouble live with April days,
> Or sadness in the summer moons?

The second is from the opening lines of *Love and Duty*:

> Of love that never found his earthly close,
> What sequel? Streaming eyes and breaking hearts?
> Or all the same as if he had not been?

LETTER LXXVI

here for tears. "Nothing is here for tears" is taken out of its context, relating to the death of Samson, from Milton's *Samson Agonistes,* line 1721.

LETTER LXXVII

the Pendulum. The lines "The Clock strikes one that just struck two" were used again later in the year, in a letter to Samuel Bowles III, to congratulate him on his engagement, with the word "Vagabond" changed to "Sorcerer" (*Letters,* p. 338).

LETTER LXXVIII

pedestrian success. "Annie's Walk on the Water." The story of Christ walking on the water is in Matthew 14:22–33.

LETTER LXXIX

but Vigor. "growing every Day, not in Grace but Vigor," II Peter 3:18 ("But grow in grace, and in the knowledge of our Lord and Saviour Jesus Christ").

trust him. "Though he slay me, yet will I trust him." Job 13:15.

LETTER LXXX

with thee. "Though thou walk through the Valley of the Shadow of Death," Psalms 23:4.

know not of. "Meat that we know not of," John 4:32.

Sheffield. A note on "Brooks of Sheffield" was given in connection with a similar allusion in Letter XVI.

Angels charge. "I give my Angels charge," Psalms 91:11.

ask or think. "more love than 'we can ask or think,'" Ephesians 3:20.

LETTER LXXXI

strange a Strength. "It is so so strange a strength" was written on the last line of one page and the first of the next, with the division coming between the two *so's.* The repetition could have been made purposely for emphasis, or it might have been accidental. In view of the uncertainty, it has seemed best to leave the second *so* in the text.

LETTER LXXXII

and the Power. "The Kingdom and the Power," Matthew 6:13 ("The Lord's Prayer").

with Hands. "not made with Hands." (See note on Letter VII).

Cathie! As a greeting to Mrs. Holland's first grandchild, whose name suggests to Emily that of the ill-fated Catherine Earnshaw in Emily Brontë's *Wuthering Heights,* she uses the despairing cry of the violent Heathcliffe when he meets the woman he loves for the last time. The sentence reads: "Oh, Cathy! Oh my life! how can I bear it?"

LETTER LXXXIII

exist in Thee. "Every existence would exist in Thee" is from Emily Brontë's poem "Last Lines," the next to last stanza:

> Though earth and man were gone
>   And suns and universes cease to be,
> And Thou wert left alone,
>   Every existence would exist in Thee.

Thomas Wentworth Higginson read the whole poem at Emily Dickinson's funeral.

first born? "the Church of the first born." Hebrews 12:23.

LETTER LXXXIV

remainder Biscuit. Emily may have remembered the words "remainder Biscuit" from a speech by Jaques in Shakespeare's *As You Like It,* Act II, Scene vii.

> O worthy fool! – One that hath been a courtier;
> And says, if ladies be but young and fair,
> They have the gift to know it: and in his brain –
> Which is as dry as the remainder biscuit
> After a voyage, – he hath strange places cramm'd
> With observation, the which he vents
> In mangled forms: –

has not foreclosed. Tommaso Salvini, whose acting of Othello had made a deep impression on Austin Dickinson, made his first appearance in the United States in the winter of 1873–1874. The following year he married an English girl, whose death three years later moved him to write: "With her the larger part of my inspiration has vanished, and I fear that I must now always remain as I am, without the hope of improving my art." In spite of his fear, he was again received with acclaim by American audiences in 1880 and 1882, and played with Edwin Booth in 1886 and 1889. *Leaves from the Autobiography of Tommaso Salvini,* from which the above quotation is taken, was published in 1883, a few months before Emily wrote this letter.

LETTER LXXXV

Stephen and I. "Stephen" may without much doubt be identified with the Steven Sullivan mentioned in *Emily Dickinson Face to Face,* p. 62, note, as one of the men who had worked for the Dickinsons. He was also probably the one described in a letter to the Misses Norcross, written in the summer of 1884 (*Letters,* p. 269): "Maggie is with us still, warm and wild and mighty, and we have a gracious boy at the barn."

Poor Cottage. "The Soul's Poor Cottage." See note on Letter XLVI.

LETTER LXXXVI

of angels. " 'seen,' we trust, 'of Angels,' " I Timothy 3:16.

secret deep. Words and phrases from her books were such a part of her, that Emily often made variations of her own, putting them in quotation marks. Such an expression is "secret deep," suggestive of biblical phraseology and of expressions used by Milton in *Paradise Lost.* In Book II, line 891, we find "The secrets of the hoary Deep," and in Book XII, lines 574–580, occurs the following passage:

> This having learned, thou hast attained the sum
> Of wisdom; hope no higher, though all the stars
> Thou knew'st by name, and all the ethereal powers,
> All secrets of the Deep, all Nature's works,
> Or works of God in heaven, air, earth, or sea,
> And all the riches of this world enjoy'st,
> And all the rule, one empire.

LETTER LXXXVIII

study of the Soudan. From 1883 through 1885 the newspapers made the world aware of the spectacular revolt of the Soudan against Anglo-Egyptian rule. Following the tragic annihilation of Hicks' army in November 1883, General Gordon was sent to the relief of the British garrison in Khartoum, where he was beseiged by the Mahdi and his followers. Throughout the summer of 1884 suspense in regard to his fate increased, and the loyalty of the Mudir of Dongola, where the British had their headquarters, was much in question. Emily must have followed the news of events from then on until the fall of Khartoum in January 1885 and the final evacuation of Dongola the following June. Several times during this period references to the Soudan occurred in her letters. It was usual for her to assimilate the news of the day and give the names she found there new values as symbols (See *Letters*, p. 421). In Letter XCIV of this series the name is used to express firm resistance, while in the present letter the suggestion is one of mystery or confusion.

LETTER XC

the Spirit. "Fruits of the Spirit," Galatians 5:22,23. ("But the fruit of the Spirit is love, joy, peace, long-suffering, gentleness, goodness, faith, meekness, temperance: against such there is no law.")

LETTER XCI

homeward flew. "The 'Swallows homeward' flew" was suggested by one of Franz Abt's popular songs, "When the swallows homeward fly," well known at that time.

Airs were delicate. In "the Airs were delicate" the swallow metaphor is carried further. It is from Shakespeare's *Macbeth,* Act I, Scene 6. Banquo is describing the scene before Macbeth's castle:

> *Banquo.* This guest of summer,
> The temple-haunting martlet, does approve
> By his loved mansionry, that the heaven's breath
> Smells wooingly here: no jutty, frieze.
> Buttress, no coign of vantage, but this bird
> Hath made his pendant bed and procreant cradle:
> Where they most breed and haunt, I have observed,
> The air is delicate.

cover it with leaves. "I did not forget the Anniversary you so tenderly marked, but cover it with leaves." This phrase seems to have been suggested by the following lines from Elizabeth Barrett Browning's *Aurora Leigh*, First Book, lines 737 and 738:

> My own self-pity, like the red-breast bird,
> Flies back to cover all that past with leaves.

LETTER XCII

despise it. Emily sometimes chose a character, real or fictitious, to act as a vehicle for a remark which seemed appropriate to the occasion. The expression "I hate it, I despise it," which she attributed to the legendary Horace, may have been his own, but Emily could have read it also in the first chapter of Henry James' novel, *The Europeans,* where it was spoken by the young baroness on arriving in Boston for the first time.

fear to touch. "The last leaf—fear to touch" is from Browning's *By the Fireside,* stanza 42.

> For a chance to make your little much,
> To gain a lover and lose a friend,
> Venture the tree and a myriad such,
> When nothing you mar but the year can mend:
> But a last leaf—fear to touch!

In this letter Emily seems to be alluding again to the meeting between Mrs. Holland and Lavinia mentioned in Letters LXXXV and LXXXVI, but since the paper on which it is written is identical with that of Letter XCIV, which belongs without question in 1885, I have dated it in February of that year instead of the previous one.

LETTER XCIV

the whole World. "To gain the whole World." Mark 8:36.

a shining Mark. In "Contention 'loves a shining mark,'" Emily has substituted the word "contention" for "death." The original passage is from Edward Young's *Night Thoughts,* Night Fifth, line 1011, and reads:

> Death loves a shining mark, a signal blow:
> A blow which, while it executes, alarms;
> And startles thousands with a single fall.

impairs my Dying. The "Dying King," whose speech is given without quotation marks, seems to be a figure of Emily's own imagining. Neither his words, nor any similar conception, has been found in the sources from which most of her quotations were taken, nor has he been identified in history, either past or contemporary.

Crowner's Quest. The expression "Crowner's quest" is from Shakespeare's *Hamlet,* Act V, Scene 1, and is used by one of the two gravediggers, who are arguing over the question whether Ophelia should have a Christian burial.

a Carpenter. "Foxes have Tenements." Matthew 8:20. ("And Jesus saith unto him, The foxes have holes, and the birds of the heaven have nests; but the Son of man hath not where to lay his head.")

LETTER XCV

no such aspect. Emily's associations with Florida were few, and in trying to picture Mrs. Holland in her new environment, her mind seems to have gone back to a series of travel letters she had read some years before in the *Springfield Republican.* They were written by George W. Stearns, a resident of Chicopee, well known in the Connecticut Valley as a brilliant lawyer and a humorist. In the issue of the third of April 1879, he described an alligator hunt, in which, at the crucial moment when the hunter was about to pull the trigger, the animal slid under the water. The phrase Emily quoted, "there was no such aspect" does not appear in Mr. Stearns' letter, but as Austin Dickinson must have known him, both professionally and as a close friend of Samuel Bowles, she might have heard the story repeated as the writer told it on his return. The phrase, however, is so characteristic of Emily herself, that this may be another instance of her habit of attributing her own words to others.

other climate grow. "The flower that never will in other climate grow" was taken from Eve's lament on leaving paradise, in Milton's *Paradise Lost,* Book ii, line 273.

O flowers
That never will in other climate grow,
My early visitation and my last
At ev'n, which I bred up with tender hand
From the first op'ning bud, and gave ye names;
Who now shall rear ye to the sun, or rank
Your tribes, and water from th' ambrosial fount?

APPENDICES

APPENDIX A

Letters Published Previously

The following table shows the dates of the twenty-nine letters which were first published in *Letters of Emily Dickinson*, as they appear in the 1931 edition of that book, and as given in this volume. For purposes of comparison, the letters are listed in the order in which I have placed them, followed by their present dates. Opposite each is the date under which it appears in *Letters*, and the page on which it is to be found. Mrs. Todd grouped a few of the letters together as belonging to a certain period, without affixing a date to each individually. For these I have taken the dates from the page headings where they occur, and placed them in brackets. The dates placed in parentheses are taken from Mrs. Todd's text introducing letters in cases where the dating called for an explanation.

I.	Autumn 1853?	[1853]	p. 156
II.	2 January 1854	January 2, 1854	p. 159
III.	Early 1854?	Late autumn, 1853	p. 157
IV.	Mid-May 1854	Spring, 1854	p. 160
V.	September 1854	About 1853	p. 155
VI.	November 1854	November, 1854	p. 161
VII.	20? January 1856	1855	p. 162
VIII.	Early August 1856?	Late summer, 1856	p. 164
IX.	November 1858	Autumn, 1876	p. 173
X.	Late March 1859	[1850–1853]	p. 153
XI.	Early summer 1859?	(Probably about 1861)	p. 169
XII.	September 1859	Autumn, 1859	p. 167
XIII.	8? December 1859	1859	p. 167
XV.	December 1859?	[1864?]	p. 171

XVII.	1860	1860	p. 168
XVIII.	Early November 1865	1864?	p. 169
XIX.	Late 1865?	[1864?]	p. 171
XX.	March 1866	[1864?]	p. 170
XXI.	Early May 1866	1857?	p. 165
XXIII.	About 1867	(1877)	p. 174
XXXVII.	August 1876	August, 1879	p. 175
XLVIII.	Spring 1878	Spring 1878	p. 174
LXIII.	13? October 1881	(October, 1881)	p. 176
LXIV.	15? October 1881	(October, 1881)	p. 177
LXV.	20 October 1881	(October, 1881)	p. 176
LXVI.	Late October 1881	(October, 1881)	p. 177
LXVIII.	Mid-December 1881	On the marriage of Mrs. Holland's daughter, December 7, 1881.	p. 178
LXIX.	Christmas 1881	Christmas 1881	p. 178
XCV.	March? 1886	1883?	p. 179

APPENDIX B

Chronology of the Dickinson and Holland Families

IMPORTANT DATES IN THE LIFE OF EMILY DICKINSON AND MEMBERS OF HER FAMILY MENTIONED IN THESE LETTERS

William Austin Dickinson born	16 April 1829
Emily Elizabeth Dickinson born	10 December 1830
Lavinia Norcross Dickinson born	28 February 1833
Dickinson family moved away from homestead	1840
Emily at Mt. Holyoke Seminary	1847–1848
Emily visited Washington and Philadelphia	Spring 1854
Dickinson family returned to homestead	1855
Austin Dickinson and Susan Gilbert married	1 July 1856
Edward (Ned) Dickinson, son of Austin and Susan, born	19 June 1861
Emily in Cambridge	April–November (?) 1864
" " "	several months 1865
Martha Dickinson, daughter of Austin and Susan, born	30 November 1866
Edward Dickinson, Emily's father, died	16 June 1874
Emily Norcross Dickinson, Emily's mother, paralyzed	June 1875
Thomas Gilbert Dickinson, son of Austin and Susan, born	31 July 1875
The Reverend Charles Wadsworth died	1 April 1882
Emily Norcross Dickinson died	14 November 1882
Thomas Gilbert Dickinson died	5 October 1883
Emily Elizabeth Dickinson died	15 May 1886

IMPORTANT DATES IN THE LIVES OF DR. AND MRS. HOLLAND AND THEIR CHILDREN UP TO THE TIME OF EMILY DICKINSON'S DEATH

Josiah Gilbert Holland born	24 July 1819
Elizabeth Luna Chapin born	3 July 1823

Josiah Gilbert Holland and Elizabeth Chapin married	7 October 1845
The Hollands at Vicksburg, Mississippi	1847–1848
J. G. Holland joined the *Springfield Republican*	1849
Annie Holland born	15 September 1851
Kate Holland born	1 November 1853
J. G. Holland's first book, *History of Western Massachusetts,* published	1854
Theodore Holland born	7 December 1859
J. G. Holland's connection with *Springfield Republican* ended	1867
Holland family in Europe	May 1868–May 1870
Scribner's Monthly started	November 1870
Holland family moved to New York	1872
"Bonniecastle" built	1877
Josiah Gilbert Holland died	12 October 1881
Annie Holland married John Howe	7 December 1881
Kate Holland married Bleecker Van Wagenen	27 September 1882
Kathrina Holland Van Wagenen born	8 August 1883
Garrat Bleecker Van Wagenen born	9 February 1885

A list of titles of J. G. Holland's books, with dates of publication, is found in *Josiah Gilbert Holland in Relation to his Times*, by Harry Houston Peckham (Philadelphia, 1940), p. 213.

APPENDIX C

A Study of the Papers Used

An important aid to the dating of the letters in this book has been a study of the various kinds of paper on which the letters are written.

All the papers are white, though of various cream or bluish tones. Some of these may have been affected by the passage of time, but on the whole the papers show very few signs of deterioration. Most of them are typical note papers of the time, probably bought in bulk at the village stationer's. The great difficulty of describing the subtle variations in tone, thickness, and glaze, without resorting to comparisons which might prove more confusing than illuminating, has made it seem best to omit these qualities from my description, though they have their value when made apparent to eye and touch.

I first made a general classification according to the type of paper and noted all watermarks and other distinguishing features found on each sheet. The next step was to measure each one with the folder open and the writing right side up, regardless of the position of the watermark. I made three measurements of height, at left and right edges and center, and two of width, at top and bottom, noting the dimensions in millimeters. When enough examples of one kind were found, a comparison of their dimensions showed considerable variation, and in some cases, subdivisions could be formed by grouping papers of identical or closely similar measurements. These differences are probably the result of slight inaccuracies in the manufacturer's cutting of one lot or another bought at different times.

In cases where only one example of a paper was found, the study was of little use for my immediate purpose, but when even two or three of a kind appeared, it became helpful. Only five groups contained enough examples for subdivision, and of these one group (19) was so irregular that letters of known date, written in close succession, showed wide variations, and further classification seemed useless. Four groups, however, have been broken down into subdivisions, in most of which the height proved to be of more importance than the width, though both were observed. These four groups cover practically the whole of the last decade of Emily Dickinson's life, from 1876 to 1885.

In spite of the usefulness of this method, it is not safe to trust it alone for dating a letter. After consideration of the handwriting and the content of each letter had done their part toward a final choice of its position in the series, the paper groups, listed again in the order of this arrangement, formed a pattern that had not appeared when they were first subdivided according to size. Certain dimensions were found to be repeated after an interval in which a subdivision of another size was used, so that in the final listing of groups 17, 20, 22, and 23, subdivisions of the same size but different dates have been marked A1 and A2. In attempting to date others of Emily Dickinson's manuscripts on the basis of these findings, the dates of both subdivisions would have to be considered.

Although my study of the papers covers only a part of Emily Dickinson's life and the papers described do not represent all those she used during those years, I hope the following description may offer a little help to those who have examples of her manuscripts that are still undated. The dimensions given cover the extremes found in measurements of height and width in all examples of a group or a subdivision of a group. I have added the dates when each was used for the first and last time in this series.

1. XIV, also poem: Baffled for just a day or two. December 1859–1860?

   159.5–160×200–201.5 mm.; wove; blind embossed seal; overall measurements form rectangle 6×13 mm., long sides slightly concave, truncated corners, in center, PARIS; no watermark.

2. XVI. March 1860.

   185.5–186×245.5 mm.; wove; ruled horizontal lines printed pale blue, 8 mm. apart, on three pages of folder, fourth unruled.

3. XXIV, XXVI, XXVII. October 1870–Late November 1871.

181–181.5×230–232 mm.; wove; watermarked A. Pirie & Sons / 1866. Large caps 15 mm., small caps 12 mm., length entire name 162 mm.

4. XXII, XXV. About 1866–October 1870?

154.5×194.5 mm.; wove; edges gilt; blind embossed seal; oval, about 10×15 mm.; indistinct horizontal lines within beaded border, in center PARIS (XXV is ½ folder with torn edge, probably left over from stock used earlier).

5. XXVIII, XXIX. ? 1872–August 1872.

198–198.5×249–251.5 mm.; wove; watermarked A Pirie & Sons / 1870; large caps 17 mm., small caps 13 mm.; length entire name 160 mm.

6. XXX, XXXII, XXXIII. Early summer 1873–May 1874.

202.5–203×253.5–254.5 mm.; wove; watermarked A Pirie & Sons / 1871; large caps 17 mm., small caps 13 mm.; length entire name 160 mm.

7. XXXI. September? 1873.

179×226–227 mm.; wove; watermarked A Pirie & Sons / 1862; large caps 17 mm., small caps 13 mm., length entire name 173 mm. (writing dates letter: paper must have been left over from stock used earlier).

8. Poem: Longing is like the Seed. 1874?

203.5×253.5–254 mm.; wove; watermarked horizontal ruled lines about 9 mm. apart; between the lines A Pirie at right edge, Sons at left (whole watermark would probably show A Pirie & Sons); length of A Pirie 49 mm.

9. Poem: When Memory is full. 1874?

Fragment, right edge torn, 126 mm. wide; wove; blind embossed seal 15×16 mm.; in center a building with dome, above in arc: CONN VALLEY, below: MILLS; ruled both sides horizontal lines printed in pale blue about 8 mm. apart.

10. XXXIV. Late January 1875.

186.5×256.5 mm.; wove; watermarked horizontal and vertical lines forming squares 8.8 mm.; vertical lines stronger than horizontal.

11. Poem: Summer laid her simple Hat. 1875?

187×256.5 mm.; wove; watermarked horizontal and vertical lines forming squares 9 mm.; lines equally strong.

12. XXXV. 1875.

202.5–203×252.5–254.5 mm.; wove; lines on both sides of sheet printed in pale blue; blind embossed seal 15×16 mm., in center domed building, above in arc: C. V. MILLS; below: CONGRESS.

13. Poem: She laid her docile Crescent down. 1875?

182.5–183×228.5–228 mm.; wove; watermarked horizontal and vertical lines forming squares 8.3 mm.

14. Poem: A little Madness in the Spring. 1875?

184×239–238 mm.; wove; watermarked horizontal and vertical lines forming squares 8.8 mm.

15. XXXVI. 1876.

185–185.5×236.5–237 mm.; wove; watermarked horizontal and vertical lines forming squares 8.3 mm.; paper not cut straight with lines.

16. Poem: No Passenger was known to flee. 1878?

184.5×237–236 mm.; wove; watermarked horizontal and vertical lines forming squares 8.7×8.9 mm.

17. A1. XXXVIII, XLI. Winter 1876 1877–Early spring 1877.

204.5×254–255.5 mm.

B. XLII, XLIII, XLIV, XLV, XLVI. Late May 1877–Early 1878.

205×253.5–256 mm.

A2. XLVII, XLIX. March? 1878–June 1878.
204.5–205×254–256 mm.
Wove; no watermark.

18. XL. Early 1877.

198.5–199×251 mm.; wove; watermarked horizontal and vertical lines forming squares 9 mm.; lines not ruled exactly at right angles.

19. L, LI, LII, LIII, LIV, LV, LVI, LVII, LVIII, LIX, LX, LXI, LXII. Mid-January 1879–Late summer 1881.

201.5–203.5×249–255.5 mm.; wove; watermarked WESTON'S / LINEN / 1876; watermark blurred; large caps 18 mm., small caps 13 mm., length of WESTON'S varies 112–115 mm.

20. A1. LXVII. Late October 1881.
203.5×251.5–254 mm.
B. LXXI, LXXII, LXXIV (1), LXXVI, LXXXI. 29? October 1882–Early May 1883.
203.5–204×251–253.5 mm.
A2. LXXXVII, LXXXIX, XC, XCI, XCIII. 1 June 1884–March 1885.
203–203.5×251–253.5 mm.

Laid; vertical chain lines average 24 mm. apart; horizontal wire lines average 72 in 10 cm.; watermarked THE / AMERICAN / LINEN PAPER Dimensions: THE 13–14×41–43 mm. AMERICAN 15–18×118–121 mm. LINEN PAPER 13–15×100–105 mm.

21. LXX. Late 1881?

203.5–204×252–254 mm.; wove; no watermark.

22. A1. LXXIII. 19? December 1882.
203–203.5×253.5–254 mm.
B. LXXVII, LXXVIII, LXXIX, LXXX. 3 March 1883–Spring 1883.
202–203.5×253.5–254.5 mm.

A2. LXXXVIII. Summer? 1884.
203–203.5×254 mm.

C. XCII, XCIV. February 1885–Spring 1885.
201.5–202.5×253–253.5 mm.

Wove; tone and thickness differ from paper 21; some sheets show no watermark, others parts of widely spaced watermark WESTON'S LINEN RECORD 1881; large caps 17 mm.; small caps 12 mm.

23. A1. LXXIV (2), LXXV. After Christmas 1882–Early 1883.
206–206.5×264–264.5 mm.

B. LXXXII, LXXXIII, LXXXIV. Late September 1883–Early 1884.
206.5×264–265.5 mm.

A2. LXXXVI (1). March 1884.
206.5×264–264.5 mm.

Laid; vertical chain lines 23.8 mm. apart; horizontal wire lines average 74 in 10 cm.; watermarked [crown design] / Pure Irish Linen [script] / F.H.D. & Co; very blurred. Entire watermark about 105–145 mm.

24. LXXXV, LXXXVI (2) (3). Early 1883.
206–208×264–266.5 mm.

Laid; horizontal chain lines average 30 mm. apart; vertical wire lines average 66 in 10 cm.; no watermark.

APPENDIX D

A Study of the Handwriting

The task of rendering Emily Dickinson's manuscripts into print can be compared to trying to represent a watercolor in an engraving. The lines, the spacing, the punctuation, as well as the highly individual forms of the script, all play a part in the effect on the reader. Some manuscripts are written with a pen, others with a pencil, and all differ according to the tool used. Since the punctuation marks, aside from the commas, consist chiefly, in the penciled letters, in small dashes of various lengths, it is impossible to reproduce them exactly, yet each must be interpreted according to the meaning of the sentence. The penciled manuscripts show no sign of haste, but were as carefully composed as those written in ink. Although these belong chiefly to the years 1879–1885, there are several dating from the 1870's when the writer usually wrote with a pen. Thus it is possible to compare examples written at about the same time, showing that the sentences in the penned letters ended with a conventional period. I have therefore interpreted the short, decisive dashes at the ends of the penciled sentences as periods, whereas the longer dashes, and most of the short ones within the sentences have been retained as "en" or "em" dashes, according to their length. I have observed the characteristic use of capitals for important nouns as consistently as the variations in the handwriting make it possible to distinguish them.

Aside from the editorial aspect, this study of the handwriting has been of the greatest importance in helping to date the letters. All Emily Dickinson's editors have noticed the changes in her writing which give the manuscripts of each decade a distinct appearance. Since none of my manuscripts is from the 1850's, and only two are from 1860, I have confined my detailed study to the years from 1870 to 1885, when the last manuscript was written. A description of these changes as I have observed them follows.

During the 1860 decade the writing began to break up into separate characters, so that by 1870 only certain characteristic combinations of linked letters remained.

LINKED LETTERS:

Letter XXIV, October 1870, has twenty combinations: *al, am, an, ar, at, av, be, bl, ch, ck, cl, en, er, ew, if, in, or, ur, th.* Several of these also appear separated. After this, there is a rapid decrease in the number of linked combinations. XXIX, August 1872, has only four: *bl, ch, of, th.* Occasional vowel combinations appear until XXXIV, late January 1875. Beginning in 1876, the pencil writing has no links. Some linked *th*'s appear in every penned letter until XLVII, March 1878, and a single *ch* is found in LIX, March 1881.

The was linked until 1874. In XXXIV it is 11 times linked, 8 separated, but after that the proportion shifts to more separated than linked, though an occasional linked *the* is found in the letters written with ink up to XLVI, Summer 1878.

Of was written as a single character until XXXIV, after which a rapid change took place within about a year, and the last appearance of this form is in XLI, Spring 1877.

CHANGES IN FORMS OF LETTERS:

d. In 1870 *d* was written with a single stroke, the ascender curving back to left. Letters XXIV–XXVIII show it thus. XXIX and XXXI have one each made with two strokes, the round body and the ascender being separate. XXXII, Autumn 1873, shows more with double than single strokes. Beginning with XXXIII, May 1874, the proportion is reversed to about 7 single to 1 double in penned letters until the pen is abandoned in 1879. In pencil writing, the double stroke *d* predominates from 1876. After 1878, an occasional single stroke *d* appears, usually as the final letter of a word at the end of a line.

e. In all the manuscripts, two forms of *e* are used, open and closed, the former similar to the capital. In XXIV and XXV, there are more open than closed *e*'s. Thereafter the closed *e* predominates in varying proportions which seem to have little significance. The open *e* is usually used for an initial letter, but may appear anywhere.

f. In 1870 the letter *f* is written with two loosely made loops, the ascender to the left, the descender to the right. In XXXIII, May 1874, we find a new form, the ascender a single line, and the descender a closed loop. The shift is very rapid, the last example of the old form appearing in XLII, May 1877.

g. The form is practically the same throughout the whole period — a small round body with a short, straight descender, but in the 1880's the latter became still shorter, and for a short period it curved back to the right in varying degrees. The number of these and the degree of curve form a definite pattern from LXXX, early summer 1883 to LXXXVI, March 1884.

t. Through XXIX, 1872, the *t*'s are crossed squarely or with a stroke flying off to the right. The *t* in *the* is crossed with a sweeping line, and the habit of crossing two *t*'s (especially in *that*) with a single stroke, persisted to the end. Gradually more strokes appear at the left of the ascender. From XLII, late May 1877, through LI, October 1879, the strokes crossing and to the left are about equal, then until LVII, late summer 1881, there are more to the left than crossing, though in some letters they are about equal again through LXVII. Thereafter there are few squarely crossed, those usually final letters, and erratic variations appear, above or to the right. In 1884 and 1885 the word *to* takes a noticeable form, to be seen in XCIV.

y. Two forms are used, both of which consist of a single stroke, one with a slight double curve, the other a single straight line or one curving slightly to the right at the bottom. From 1870 to 1879 there are few straight *y*'s, sometimes in the signature and occasionally as the final letter of a word. With the beginning of the penciled letters, the final straight *y* becomes usual. Medial *y* varies, and initial *y* remains curved to the end. In 1882–1883 there are more final *y*'s with a tendency to curve to the right, and initial *y*'s develop a hooklike curve at the upper end. From L, January 1879, the signature always has a straight *y*.

CAPITALS:

H. Until 1876, the cross stroke is made by continuing the stroke at the right from the line upward in a loop and across. The first appearance of a simple block *H* made with three separate strokes is in XXXVIII. Thereafter, through XLV, early 1878, both forms appear, after which all are made with three strokes.

V. is rounded at the base until LI, October 1879, when it becomes more pointed, though both forms appear until the transformation is complete in LVIII, early 1881.

W. is rounded at the base until XXXIV, late January 1875, when the first pointed *W* appears. Occasional rounded *W*'s appear until the pen is abandoned in 1879.

SIZE AND SLANT:

The writing reaches its greatest size in 1874 and 1875, after which there is a slight diminishing. The penciled letters, beginning in 1875, show a smaller and more precise writing with less slant than the pen writing. By 1881, the pencil writing begins to slant more and increase in size, with less space between the lines. LXXXVII, 1 June 1884, marks the beginning of a change toward larger, less well-formed writing, in which some of the letters are practically recumbent.

NOTES ON REPRODUCTIONS:

The manuscripts of the letters in this book are now in the Emily Dickinson Collection at Harvard University. The following reproductions of pages from them have been selected to illustrate the changes outlined here, and the notes for each indicate the special points to be observed in them that distinguish the writing at the time they were written. In each case the reproduction is about four-fifths the size of the original.

1

XXIV, p. 4. October 1870. Ink. Linked letters: *an, ar, av, er, ey, un, ur, fe, th*; capital *W* rounded at base; capital *H* made with two strokes; *d* made with single stroke, ascender curving to right; open and closed *e*; cross stroke of *t* across ascender, to right, and sweeping above; straight *y* exceptional at this date.

2

XXXII, p. 3. Autumn 1873. Ink. Linked letters: *bl, fe*; both linked and separated: *th, ar, er, ev; d* made with two strokes; curved *y*; cross strokes of *t* across, left, or sweeping. Word *of* linked in special form, showing *f* without loops.

3

XXXIV, p. 3. Late January 1875. Ink. Maximum size of writing. Only linked combinations *of, th* (occasional *er* on other pages). New form of *f*, ascender straight, descender looped; *d* made with single stroke.

4

XXXV, p. 1. 1875? Pencil. No linked combinations except *bl* and *of*. Both kinds of *d*; both kinds of *y*—curved and straight. General appearance approximates script in slant and flowing effect.

5

XL, p. 1. Early spring 1877. Pencil. Writing smaller, less slanting, wide spaces between lines; first capital *W* with pointed base; only one linked *th*; both forms of *d*; two *y*'s curved, two straight. Facsimiles 5 and 6 show contrast between pen and pencil writing at the same time.

6

XLI, p. 1. Early spring 1877. Ink. No linked letters except two *th*'s; *of* separated, using new form of *f* in use since XXXIV; capital *H* made with three straight strokes.

7

XLVI, p. 1. Early 1878. Ink. Only one linked *th*; first capital *W* in ink with pointed base; two kinds of *d* in same proportion; larger proportion of cross strokes of *t* to left of ascender than in XL and XLI, though still less than half.

8

LI, p. 3. October 1879. Pencil. Smaller, freer effect than earlier pencil writing; capitals smaller; capital *V* sharper at base; all *d*'s made with two strokes – after this the single stroke form appears seldom, usually at end of line; more than half the cross strokes of *t* to left of ascender. Initial *y* curved; final *y* straight.

9

LXXI, p. 3. 29? October 1882. Pencil. Letters less rounded, narrower, more slanting; most cross strokes of *t* to left of ascender; initial *y* curves over into hook at top; final *y* shows tendency to curve back to right at lower tip. This page gives a good example of long and short dashes used in pencil writing.

10

LXXXIII, p. 1. November? 1883. Pencil. Very slanting, hurried effect. Descenders of *y* and *g* curved violently back to right; cross strokes of *t* mostly very short, detached, to left.

11

LXXXVI, p. 2. March 1884. Pencil. End of period in which *g*'s curve back to right; cross strokes of *t* very low, detached, to left of ascender; ascender of *d* very low – hardly distinguishable from *a*.

12

XCIV, p. 4. Spring 1885. Pencil. Extreme slant; letters out of alignment; some, like *t*, lying almost horizontal above the line; *to* has become conventionalized sign; descender of *g* very short and straight; no cross strokes of *t* cross ascender.

To shut our Eyes
is Travel.
The Seasons
understand this.
How lonesome to
be an Article!
I mean - to have
no soul.
An Apple fell
in the Night
and a Wagon
stopped.
I suppose the
Wagon ate the
Apple. and resumed
it's way.

Enrichment.
It puts me in
mind of that
singular Verse
in the Revelations,
"Every several
Gate was of
one Pearl."
Little Sister -
Good Night -
I am sure
you went.
Parting is
one of the
Exactions of
a Mortal Life.
It is bleak.

The Masked
Bed - in The
Marl House.
How soft his
Prison is -
How sweet
those sullen
Bars -
No Despot -
but The King
of Down
Invented that
Repose!
When I Think
of his firm
Light - quenched

Sister -
I have the
little Book and
am twice triumphant -
Once for itself,
And once for those
who enabled me.
the embarrassment
of the Psalmist
who knew not
what to render
his friend - is
peculiarly mine.
Though he has
canceled his
Consternations while
my own remain -
thank you with
all my strength.

35

Will my little Sister
Excuse me?
"Houglass, Houglass,
tender and true"
who never swindled
me! I am ashamed
and sorry. I meant
hypothetic tomorrows –
though are there
any other?

(40)

Sister.
The vitality
of your Syllables
compensates
for their
infrequency.
There is not
so much Life
as talk of
Life, as a
general thing.
Had we the
first intimation
of the Definition
of Life, the
calmest of us

(41)

Dear Doctor,

We rejoice in your repaired health, though it grieves us that repairs should be necessary in a structure so able. Yet when we recall that the "Soul's poor Cottage, battered and dismayed, lets in new light through

Crevices"

46

It will rivet us
to your remembrance
to tell you that
Austin and Sue
have just returned
from Belchertown
Cattle Show -
Austin brought me
a Balloon and
Vinnie a Watermelon
and each of his
family a Whip -
Wasn't it primitive?
When they drove
away in the dust
this morning, I told
them they looked
like Mr and Mrs

(51)

could not pass
you by -
It sometimes seems
as if special
Months gave and
took away -
August has
brought the most
to me - April -
robbed me most -
in incessant
instances -
Your Brother bore
a strong re-
semblance to a
Childhood's friend
who long since
died, and whose

(71)

Sweet Sister -

Was that
what I used to
call you?
I hardly recollect.
All seems so
different -
I hesitate which
word to take, as
I can take but
few and each
must be the chiefest,
but recall that
Earth's most graphic
transaction is placed
within a syllable,
nay, even a gaze -

us, he hastened
and, "seen," we trust,
"of Angels" - who
knows that secret,
deep in "Alas, not I.
Forgive the Tears
that fell for few.
but that fell too
many, for was not
each a World?
Your last dear
words seemed
stronger, and
smiling in the
feeling that you
were to be, this
latest sorrow came.
I have seen own

sat in the Sun
that the Little
Boy in the
Trinity had no
Grandmama, only
a Holy Ghost.
But you must
go to sleep.
I, who sleep
always, need
no Bed.
Foxes have
Tenements, and
remember, the
Speaker was
a Carpenter.

Emily.

INDEX OF POEMS

The following abbreviations are used in this index: *Poems* = *The Poems of Emily Dickinson; Letters* = *Letters of Emily Dickinson; F. F.* = *Emily Dickinson Face to Face; Bolts* = *Bolts of Melody*

The poems on the first and last pages of this book are not among those which Emily Dickinson sent to the Hollands. They may be found as follows:

GENERAL INDEX